onme

By Mark Crutcher

International Standard Book Number: 0-9648886-1-0

LIFE DYNAMICS INCORPORATED

Introduction

Recent polls show that this is a time of unprecedented opportunity for the pro-life movement. The public is having profound second-thoughts about abortion and more people are labeling themselves pro-life than at any other point in our history. Better yet, this trend is especially strong among the young—and it's growing.

Meanwhile, our opposition is having a much more difficult time selling their agenda, and we are even starting to see a few cracks in the media's and Democratic Party's support for abortion. Also, the number of abortion clinics in America is plummeting. From a high of more than 2000 in the early 1990s, there are only about 750 remaining today with more closing almost every month. That has resulted in a significant drop in the number of children killed.

The bottom line is, we not only command the moral high-ground but we have the momentum as well. However, this is not a time to relax. This is the time to educate the new people coming into our movement and re-educate our veterans. The pro-life struggle is a grass-roots campaign that will be won by people talking to their friends, relatives, co-workers and neighbors. To capitalize on the opportunities now before us, belief and commitment alone are not enough. Our people must be knowledgeable, uncompromising, and consistent. In other words, each of us has to stay...

onmessage.

The Foundation

No one can be an effective advocate for the unborn without a complete understanding of the fundamental principle guiding the pro-life position. The good news is, it's actually a very easy position to understand.

"Pro-Life" is the belief that (a) human life begins at the moment a woman's egg is fertilized by a man's sperm, and (b) every human being is entitled to have his or her life protected by law from that moment forward.

Regrettably, the pro-life position is often compromised or watered-down for political expediency or in a misguided effort to appear "reasonable." You'll hear people say that they are pro-life but that there should be "exceptions" for certain circumstances. The most common exceptions given are for pregnancies which threaten the mother's life or health, when the pregnancy resulted from either rape or incest, or when the unborn child is handicapped. Some people—especially politicians—will even claim to be pro-life while openly stating that abortion should be legal in the first trimester. (Arguments against each of these exceptions are provided in the **ISSUES AND ANSWERS** section of this book.)

To see what a fraud these "exceptions" positions are, simply paraphrase them. For example, the statement, "I am pro-life, but I think there should be an exception when the pregnancy was the result of rape" should become, "I am pro-life, but it should be legal to butcher babies who were conceived in rape." Other paraphrased positions would be, "I am pro-life, but it should be legal to butcher babies with Down's syndrome" and "I am pro-life, but I think it is okay to butcher babies in their first trimester of life."

onmessage

Every exception can be paraphrased to more accurately reflect what is actually being said, and in doing so it becomes clear that ...

THERE IS NO SUCH POSITION AS
"PRO-LIFE WITH EXCEPTIONS."

By definition, it is impossible to accurately label someone pro-life who approves killing certain groups of children. It is as illogical as someone in 1860 saying, "I am an abolitionist but I believe slavery should be legal in some circumstances."

Remember, the only legitimate pro-life position is that a 10-week-old unborn child is morally equivalent to, and has the same right to life as, a five-year-old born child. When someone says they are pro-life but that abortion should be allowed in some circumstances, the question is whether they would support killing a five-year-old in those same circumstances. Since they are certainly not going to take that position, the only logical conclusion is that they don't see born and unborn children as morally equal. In other words, they are not pro-life.

The bottom line is, when someone says they are "Pro-life with exceptions" what they are saying is that they support the "choice" to kill some babies (conceived in rape, handicapped, etc.) but oppose the "choice" to kill other babies. In other words, the only honest way to define their position is ...

"PRO-CHOICE WITH EXCEPTIONS."

The Rules

Later in this book, you will find responses to the toughest issues abortion defenders can raise. However, being an effective advocate for the unborn child requires more than memorizing answers to the standard pro-abortion arguments. You have to understand the basic rules for responding to issues raised by abortion advocates. With that knowledge, you will be able to effectively answer any question whether you've heard it before or not.

The key to success is "thinking like a pro-lifer" not just *being* a pro-lifer. To reach that level, you first need to comprehend a few simple rules. Through them you can learn how to **RESPOND** to pro-abortion issues rather than simply **REACT** to them, and in that distinction lies the difference between winning and losing. It's the same as taking medicine ...

REACTING IS BAD — RESPONDING IS GOOD.

TREAT EVERY DISCUSSION SERIOUSLY

There are no unimportant discussions about abortion. First, with the public's growing unease over abortion, people who we could have never reached in the past are at least willing to listen to the pro-life message. Even among abortion clinic employees, there is a creeping sense of doubt about what they are doing. Morale is low, turnover rates are astronomical, discouragement is rampant, and while they would never admit it, every rational pro-life argument they hear amplifies their doubts.

Second, even if we think the American people are not interested in our message, we have an obligation to constantly hold their sin in front of them. No American should ever draw even one comfortable breath as long as we are legally butchering God's children. That environment can only be created through sound and aggressive pro-life responses which expose the flaws and distortions in abortion industry double-speak.

The final reason to take every discussion on abortion seriously is what I call the "Note in a Bottle" phenomenon. Imagine that you are stranded on a desert island. You find a bottle, put a note in it and toss it in the ocean hoping that someone will find it and rescue you. With the realization that what is written on that note may be your only hope for survival, you are probably going to write a pretty thorough and compelling message. That same attitude should be your guiding principle anytime you are discussing abortion. Always assume that the words you are using will one day be repeated to a pregnant woman who is considering abortion. It may not happen for years, and you may never know about it, but there is a reasonable probability of this happening. When it does, the message you gave may be the only hope that baby has for survival.

RECOGNIZE THE CUSTOMER

When you articulate the pro-life message to another person, you are in effect participating in a marketing battle. You are selling the concept that unborn children have the right not to be killed.

In marketing, the primary requirement is to identify who your customer is. The best marketing strategy in the world will not work if it is directed toward someone who is either incapable of buying the product or unwilling to even consider buying it. As any marketing expert will tell you, the fishing lure company which designs its lures to catch fish will be put out of business by the company that designs its lures to catch fishermen.

onmessage

In this marketing environment, the first thing to understand is that "True Believers" are not customers. The people who are 100% locked into either camp cannot be won or lost. Someone who is solidly pro-life can watch an abortion debate in which the pro-life side gets absolutely pummeled and it will not change their opinion one bit. The opposite is also true. If the pro-lifer is the clear winner, anyone who was a hardcore pro-abort when the debate started was still a hardcore pro-abort when it ended.

There are those who will argue that this is not true by pointing out that some very high-profile pro-lifers were at one time outspoken pro-aborts, and that is true. However, it is the exception. If you go back 20 years and identify all the Americans who could have been accurately described as being hardcore pro-aborts, today virtually all of those people are still hardcore pro-aborts. Moreover, those who have "come over" generally did so because of a personal experience they had or because of something they saw in the abortion industry. Those who changed their minds because of something a pro-lifer said are extraordinarily rare.

For customer identification purposes, the public can be divided according to the following bar graph:

10	9 • 8 • 7 • 6 • 5 • 4 • 3 • 2 • 1	0

The "10's" are the hardcore pro-lifers and the "0's" are the hardcore pro-aborts. **The "9-1" block is your customer base.** Don't worry about the "10's" because you can't lose them. Unless you just need the practice, don't waste your time with the "0's" unless there are some "customers" within earshot.

7

onmessage

ACCEPT THAT YOU HAVE SOME DISADVANTAGES

In the abortion battle, the pro-life position is, naturally, the harder one to sell. Most Americans are not good conceptual thinkers and we are asking them to accept that some "entity" has Constitutional rights which (a) they can't normally see, (b) they cannot interact with, and (c) is incredibly small for the first part of its life. Of course, ultrasound does give people the ability to see the unborn, but that does not necessarily alter their position on abortion. That may be because they already believe the unborn are human, or because they are less impressed with the images they see than they are with the technology that enabled them to see those images.

Another problem is that, on some very simplistic level, the pro-life position appears to conflict with the concepts of personal liberty and individual freedom in which most Americans believe. That is why the "Pro-Choice" marketing slogan has been so successful.

Fortunately, these challenges are **not** deal-breakers.

KNOW YOUR OPPONENT'S STRATEGIES

Study their rhetoric and one thing becomes crystal clear. Although abortion defenders have a sizeable catalogue of rhetorical tools, a significant percentage revolve around just five basic strategies:

> **STRATEGY 1:** Never defend the actual act of abortion and avoid even talking about it if at all possible. Only defend the right of someone to have an abortion.

> **RESPONSE:** Our job is to neutralize their diversionary language and force them to tell the public why abortion itself is such a good thing. That is a battle which our opponents know they cannot win.

8

STRATEGY 2: Sell the idea that abortion is a solution to social problems (child abuse, hunger, homelessness, etc.).

> **RESPONSE:** We must constantly remind the public that every social problem we faced the day abortion became legal is far worse now than it was then.

STRATEGY 3: Emotionally blackmail the public by lying about the horror stories that will result from prohibiting abortion. The most common is their suggestion that if we outlaw abortion we won't be able to walk down any street in America without having to step over the bloody corpses of women killed by illegal abortions.

> **RESPONSE:** The American people seem to have forgotten that abortion was at one time illegal and that these horror stories which the abortion lobby says will be so common were actually quite rare and in some cases non-existent. Our job is to remind them.

STRATEGY 4: Sell abortion as a women's rights issue.

> **RESPONSE:** We've got to do a better job of showing that the historic feminist position on abortion is pro-life. Early feminists almost universally denounced abortion as something that devalues women and makes them easier for sexually irresponsible and sexually predatory males to exploit.

STRATEGY 5: Never argue that the unborn isn't human. Instead, segregate them from the rest of humanity and convince the public to apply different standards to unborn human beings than they apply to all other human beings.

> **RESPONSE:** It is not enough to simply establish the humanity of the unborn. Polls consistently show that the vast majority of the American people already

believe the unborn child is a living human being, so our rhetoric must always reflect the principle that there is no difference between born and unborn people. Whatever excuse is used to justify abortion, we apply to killing the born.

We must show the American people the hypocrisy of believing that the unborn are human, but allowing them to be slaughtered at the same time we insist that our own lives be protected by law. For example, if someone defends abortion for children with Down's syndrome, our response should include language about killing born children with Down's syndrome. The fundamental question is: why are unborn children the only class of innocent human beings that it should be legal to butcher by the millions?

IDENTIFY GOALS AND ASSUMPTIONS

There is no piece of information which we have and our opponents don't have. This means that, with virtually no exceptions, their questions are not asked in order to gain information, but to lure us into saying something which undermines the pro-life position. In other words, their questions always have a specific goal. Without identifying that goal, it is impossible to give a winning response.

> **EXAMPLE:** "If we outlaw abortion, who is going to pay for all these unwanted children?"

The goal of this question is to make the public fear that prohibiting abortion will cost them money. They want people to think that they will be paying for all the children who are not aborted. If your answer includes rhetoric about government welfare programs or charities raising money for the poor, **you lose**. Just remember, when you answer a question as if it were asked to gain information, you are **reacting** to the question. When you answer in a way that denies your opponent the goal they sought, you are **responding**.

Also be aware that almost every issue an abortion defender will raise is based on an assumption that is untrue. Their goal is to get that assumption heard without it being challenged. Using the question above as an example, it assumes, (a) that there will be more unwanted children, (b) that all unaborted pregnancies produce unwanted babies, (c) that every woman who is denied the ability to have an abortion will have to be given financial help in order to raise her child. Everytime the public hears those assumptions without a challenge, the abortion lobby profits— **regardless of how we answer the question**. The advantage we have is that when their untrue assumptions are exposed, the issue inevitably favors us.

DON'T REINFORCE THEIR ARGUMENTS

Unknowingly, pro-lifers often use rhetoric that reinforces pro-abortion positions. For example, when we focus on the horrible and indefensible nature of late term abortion, we are suggesting that earlier abortions are less horrible and more defensible. In effect, we are saying that there is a difference between one human being and another human being, based on how old it is, how developed it is or how large it is. Subtly, we are implying that the more it looks like us the more entitled it is to be protected.

Remember, the pro-life position is that life begins at conception. When we suggest that there is a distinction between killing a first trimester baby, a third trimester baby, or a five-year-old child, we surrender credibility. This is another reason why we cannot support any exceptions or compromises to the right to life.

Another example of how we reinforce the pro-abortion position relates to the revelations that some hospitals are doing what are called "live birth abortions." This is where they induce a pregnant woman to give birth and then put the baby in a closet and let it die. Horrified pro-lifers have responded by talking about the fact that these hospitals are "killing living babies!" But, as understandable as this outrage is, this language undermines the pro-life position. It suggests that there is a difference between killing someone inside the womb or outside. The reality is, whether they are put in closets to die or ripped apart in the womb, **all elective abortions happen on living babies** and we must be careful not to ever say or do anything which suggests otherwise.

Another way we get tricked into supporting the abortion lobby's agenda is in the way we talk about teen pregnancy. The abortion industry wants people to believe that when a teenage girl has a baby her life is over. She is doomed to be single forever, poor as a church mouse, uneducated, and on welfare for the rest of her life. Their goal is to convince people that abortion is her only hope.

The fact is, many unmarried teenage girls have babies and go on to lead happy lives. Moreover, among those who don't, a significant number come from socio-economic environments where, by abortion industry standards, their chances for a "successful and productive" life are limited whether they have babies or not. For these girls, the problem is not their baby but their environment.

Obviously, no one believes that 13-year-old single girls should be getting pregnant. But when they do, **it is not the end of the world**. In fact, when an unmarried girl or woman is pregnant, the problem is that she and the person who got her pregnant were engaged in a sinful sexual relationship. When we ignore that, and focus instead on the pregnancy, what we are really saying is that the baby is the problem. Again, that's the pro-abortion position.

It is also common for pro-lifers to attack abortion by saying we may have aborted the next Beethoven, or Mother Teresa, or the doctor who would have discoverd a cure for cancer. While this sentiment is understandable, it is inconsistent with the pro-life position. The unborn child who might grow up to cure cancer has no more right to life than the unborn child who will spend his life on welfare and living under bridges. The "aborted Beethoven" argument suggests that it is a bigger tragedy to kill Baby A than Baby B because Baby A is more valuable to society. Clearly, that is not what the pro-lifer meant to say, but that is certainly what the listener might conclude.

CONTROL THE LANGUAGE

Over the years, we have seen that the abortion lobby is extremely skilled at twisting language to suit their agenda. They understand that the rhetoric used often makes the difference between winning and losing. While we cannot force them to change their language, when we expose the deceit in their rhetoric we expose the deceit in their entire argument. The following are a few examples:

What gives you the right to tell a woman she can't terminate her pregnancy?

The Flaw: We're not trying to tell women they cannot terminate their pregnancies. All pregnancies terminate. The only thing we're trying to insure is that they terminate with a live baby rather than a dead baby. In an abortion, it is a baby that gets terminated. That's what we want to stop. But we're certainly not stupid enough to think that we can stop pregnancy terminations.

What about a 15-year-old girl who finds herself pregnant?

The Flaw: No 15-year-old girl ever "found" herself pregnant. They get pregnant and it is not an insult to women to say that. One major abortion industry strategy has been to project women as victims of their pregnancies and this sort of deceptive rhetoric is a crucial element in that effort. Their thinking is that it is much easier to justify abortions for women who are victims of their pregnancies rather than participants in them.

onmessage

You have no right to tell a woman she has to have a child.

The Flaw: No one in the pro-life movement has ever suggested that women be required to have children. We don't go marauding around the countryside dragging non-pregnant women in and insisting that they get pregnant. However, when a woman is pregnant it is a biological fact that she already has a child. Our position is that she should not be allowed to murder that child.

Women must not be denied the right to control their own reproductive lives.

The Flaw: We have absolutely no interest in controlling women's reproductive lives. However, the biological reality is that when a woman is pregnant, reproduction has already occurred. If that were not true, there would be nothing for the abortionist to kill.

What gives you people the right to deny women access to healthcare?

The Flaw: Abortion is not healthcare. Healthcare relates to the treatment of diseases, injuries or illnesses. Since pregnancy is none of those, abortion cannot be healthcare.

We have a nation full of babies having babies.

The Flaw: Why is it that a pregnant 14-year-old who wants to have her baby is called "a baby having a baby," while a 14-year-old who submits to an abortion is called "a young woman exercising her Constitutional rights?" Why don't we hear the abortion industry referring to these girls as "babies having abortions" or "babies killing babies?"

This is clearly just a sleazy effort by the abortion industry to market abortion as some bizarre right of passage. If you're 14 and having a baby, you're just a baby having a baby, but if you're 14 and willing to submit to an abortion, you're a young woman.

NOTE: I used the word "submit" in the previous paragraph. This is an important language issue. The abortion industry wants to sell this image of abortion as something which empowers women. That is a lie. To make sure that people see it for exactly what it is, always refer to abortion as something women submit to, not something they have.

Are you going to have the baby?

The Flaw: When a woman is pregnant, she has no choice but to "have the baby." The only thing to be decided is whether she will have a live baby or a dead baby.

She is just not ready to be a mom.

The Flaw: Ready or not, if she's pregnant she is a mom. The only question is, will she choose to be the mother of a living baby or a dead one. At this point, those are the only options she has.

Why don't you people do something to help people who are already here?

The Flaw: Unborn children are already here. If that were not the case there would be nothing for the abortionist to kill. What we're trying to do is insure that they are allowed to remain here in the same way the rest of us were allowed to remain here. Alive.

Pro-Abortion or Pro-Choice

Although I have consistently trained pro-lifers that we should never use the term pro-choice to describe our opponents or their position, I now see that using this term can, in some circumstances, actually benefit us.

First, regardless of anything we do or say, we will never be able to make the public, or the media, or Hollywood, or anyone else quit using the term pro-choice. Given that reality, our best strategy is to "toxify" the term. Our goal is to turn "choice" into a four-letter word.

In this effort, we can take a lesson from our opponents. Notice that they normally refer to us as "anti-choice extremists" or something similar. But if an abortionist is shot, or there is some other kind of violence, or a pro-lifer does something illegal, suddenly they call us pro-life. This is not by accident. They are degrading the term pro-life by linking it to something bad, and over the years they've done a very good job of this. They figured out a long time ago that it is good strategy to associate the term "pro-life" with negative images.

That same strategy is available to us. When one of our responses negatively impacts the term "pro-abortion," it does us little good since almost no one considers themselves pro-abortion. But when we expose the purposeful deceit and flaws in our opponents' arguments, or when they do something bad or outrageous, we are far better off if we can make it reflect on "choice" rather than directly on abortion. Obviously, that can only happen if we use the term "pro-choice" in those circumstances rather than pro-abortion.

Second, as mentioned earlier, a fundamental strategy of the abortion lobby is to avoid having to defend or, if possible, even talk about abortion. When we call them pro-abortion, we allow them to divert attention away from the abortion issue itself by tying us up in an argument about whether they are pro-choice or pro-abortion. Meanwhile, the time spent in this relatively meaningless argument is stolen from the far more important discussion about killing children. That is precisely what our opponents want.

Third, remember the customer identification bar graph shown earlier in this book. When we automatically label anyone who isn't pro-life as pro-abortion, we drive a wedge between us and many of the people on that graph. The irony is, the people we are most likely to alienate are the ones who should be the easiest for us to win over. If someone is a 7, or an 8, or a 9, they do not consider themselves pro-abortion and they are offended if we suggest they are. For us, that is not a formula for success. Also, even if we give a response that destroys a "pro-abortion" argument, these people do not see that as relative to their position since they do not consider themselves pro-abortion. To them, we're talking about some radical who is out on the fringes of the abortion movement.

Fourth, the abortion industry has so overused the word "choice" that most people now recognize that it is simply a code word for abortion. The result is that "choice" is losing its ability to insulate the abortion lobby from abortion. Additionally, the public's growing discomfort over legalized abortion may be partly driven by their observation that even people who defend it are so adamant that they not be identified with it. When we reinforce that "choice" is just a code word for abortion, we remind them of this fact.

Finally, I am not suggesting that we universally abandon the term "pro-abortion" for the term "pro-choice." What I'm saying is that we should be willing to use "pro-choice" strategically. We should use it when it would benefit the pro-life cause more than using "pro-abortion" would. As difficult a change as this might be for some of us (especially me), we have to honestly answer whether we want to use rhetoric that is effective or rhetoric that makes us feel good.

Issues and Answers

The issue is not whether abortion is right or wrong but who decides, the woman or the government. We are not pro-abortion, we are pro-choice.

From day one, abortion advocates have understood that the actual act of abortion is indefensible. Their response has been to contend that whether abortion is the deliberate killing of a living human being or not is a separate issue from whether it should be legal. As irrational as it is, this is the only strategy they have yet devised to insulate themselves from the immorality of the activity which they advocate. They have to divert public attention toward the philosophical concepts of "Choice" and "Who Decides" because they can't afford for the public to look at what's being decided.

Defenders of slavery used this same strategy. During the Abraham Lincoln-Stephen Douglas debates of 1858, Douglas maintained that even though he was personally opposed to slavery he would not legislate against it. He said it was up to the people to decide. Lincoln countered by saying:

> *"He cannot say that he would as soon see a wrong voted up as voted down. When Judge Douglas says whoever, or whatever community, wants slaves, they have a right to them, he is perfectly logical if there is nothing wrong in the institution; but if you admit that it is wrong, he cannot logically say that anybody has a right to do a wrong."*

The analogy between abortion and slavery is seen in the following statement made by Stephen Douglas defending his pro-choice position on slavery:

onmessage

"I am now speaking of rights under the Constitution, and not of moral or religious rights. I do not discuss the morals of the people favoring slavery, but let them settle that matter for themselves. I hold that the people who favor slavery are civilized, that they bear consciences, and that they are accountable to God and their posterity and not to us. It is for them to decide therefore the moral and religious right of the slavery question for themselves within their own limits."

Just substitute the word "abortion" every place the word "slavery" appears and this statement perfectly defines the pro-choice position in America today. Apparently, those who defend evil always rely upon the same rhetoric, regardless of the evil they're trying to defend.

•••

Before one can rightly claim that the issue is "Choice" or "Who Decides" one must first examine what's being chosen. If it's what color shoes to wear, that's one thing. If it's whether to kill another human being, that's another. Except in self-defense, the decision about whether one human being can kill another should never be left up to the individual who wants to do the killing.

•••

Simply because America is a country dedicated to the idea of individual rights, does not mean we allow each person to do absolutely anything they want to do. There is nothing intrinsically noble about the concept of choice. There are many choices, personal and otherwise, which a society cannot allow the individual to make. Total freedom for each individual to choose to do anything he or she wishes is anarchy.

•••

When people participate in a socio-political movement, you don't see them desperately trying to avoid being linked to the activity with which the movement is identified. For example, those who support the death penalty don't mind being called pro-death penalty. People who work for animal rights don't mind being called pro-animal rights. People for federal child care don't mind being called pro-child care. Those who support the Equal Rights

19

Amendment don't mind being called pro-ERA. People who support the Second Amendment don't mind being called pro-gun, and the list goes on and on. The exception is people who support legal abortion. At the same time they viciously defend abortion's legality, they rail at being labeled pro-abortion. Clearly, they are advocating the legality of an activity which even they know is indefensible. If that were not the case they would not become so outraged at being called pro-abortion.

•••

As used by abortion advocates, the term "pro-choice" is both inaccurate and dishonest. To begin with, when an abortion takes place at least three people are directly impacted, including the mother, the father, and the child. Abortion advocates say only one is entitled to a choice. Also, it has never been a part of their agenda to protect any choice other than abortion. They don't lobby for women to have the legal right to be prostitutes or use crack cocaine. Yet these laws, and thousands of others, restrict the right of women to choose what to do with their bodies just as much as laws preventing abortion would.

Furthermore, the abortion industry has always fought tooth and nail against any attempt to pass legislation which would reduce America's staggering abortion rate. They have spent millions lobbying against legislation to make sure women are fully informed before submitting to abortion, laws that require parents to be notified before their underage daughters can submit to abortions, requirements to make abortion clinics meet the same medical standards as legitimate health care providers, and short waiting periods designed to give women the opportunity to be sure they are making the choice that's right for them.

Given the fact that not one of these measures would deny even one woman the ability to choose abortion, people who claim to oppose them because they interfere with "A Woman's Right to Choose" are simply lying. The fact is, the abortion lobby opposes even the most insignificant and reasonable limits on abortion, not because they reduce choices but because they reduce abortions.

•••

Saying that the question of abortion is a matter of "who decides the woman or the state" is asinine. Laws against abortion would not let the state decide who gets abortions any more than laws against rape let the state decide who gets raped. Such a law would simply establish that abortion is murder and, therefore, illegal.

•••

It's interesting that the only people claiming that it doesn't matter whether abortion is right or wrong are those who support it. The question is, if they think legalized abortion is such a good thing why won't they defend it on its own merits? The answer, of course, is that it has no merits. There is nothing especially appealing about a woman lying on a table while a man invades her body with sharp instruments in order to rip her child apart. When it is over, the most notable accomplishment has been that the mother of a live baby has been turned into the mother of a dead one.

The government has no right to interfere in someone's personal choices.

The question of whether government has the right to restrict choices is not logical. Restricting choices is precisely what laws do. By definition, every law is intended to deny someone the legal ability to choose a particular activity. While it sounds good to say that government should allow people to make all of their own choices, that is neither practical nor desirable.

The reality is, all choices are not created equal. Some choices are crimes. All crimes are choices. We do not let people make their own choices to rape, rob or drive drunk. We do not let them make the choices to embezzle, defraud, write hot checks, drive their cars over the speed limit, slander other people, etc. Some choices we prohibit could even be considered "personal decisions." For example, it is illegal to have sexual relations with a sibling, or a child, or an animal, or a dead body. The list is endless, but the point is that simply calling a decision "personal" does not make it off-limits to the law.

•••

It is not the government's role to protect one individual's right to victimize another. There will always be people who make conscious decisions to victimize other people, and the government has an obligation to stop them.

•••

If there is only one legitimate function of government, it is the protection of innocent human life. If the unborn is a living human being, then taking that life is no different than taking the life of any other living human being. No government can justify allowing the unborn to be lawfully killed at the discretion of their mothers unless it has first established that the unborn are not living human beings. To pretend as if the humanity of the unborn is irrelevant is both legally and morally indefensible. If government has a responsibility to keep one individual from killing another, then the real question is not whether the government has the right to take action against abortion, but whether it has the right not to.

•••

The very people who are the most adamant that the government should stay out of the abortion decision are the same ones who say the government should pay for abortions. In other words, the pro-choice position is that, (a) abortion is a "private and personal" decision and society has no right to tell a woman she can't kill her unborn child, and (b) if a woman chooses abortion, even taxpayers who believe abortion is murder should have no choice but to pay for it. It takes a lot of nerve to tell the public that something is none of their business, then grab their wallets to pay for it.

The government has no right to come into our bedrooms.

Questions like this are designed to scare the public into thinking that making abortion illegal is a "threshold issue" and opens the door for more government meddling into their private lives. This fear assumes two things which are demonstrably untrue. First, that abortion is a bedroom issue, and second, that the bedroom is off-limits to the law. Of course, the first assumption is laughable given that abortions are not performed in bedrooms.

As for the second assumption, simply because something occurs in a bedroom does not make it beyond the legitimate scope of the law. Many illegal acts happen in bedrooms. In fact, some illegal activities (spousal abuse, incest, pedophilia, etc.) usually occur in bedrooms. However, that does not mean that the perpetrators are insulated against legal consequences. The bedroom has never been and should never become an impenetrable sanctuary from the law. Let's also not forget that when abortion was illegal, law-abiding Americans were at no greater risk of having their bedrooms invaded by the state than they are today.

•••

Societies have always enacted laws to deal with activities that occur in bedrooms. If a fifty-year-old man lures a 12-year-old girl into having sex with him, should he be indicted if the act occurred in a car but not if it occurred in a bedroom? If a man beats his wife, should it be legal in their bedroom but illegal in their living room?

The reality is that when lawmakers are considering whether an activity should be legal or not, where it occurs is seldom a factor. In this case, abortion is a crime against humanity whether it is committed in a hospital, a bedroom or a cornfield. Whatever the environment, abortion is the intentional murder of an innocent human being and should not be tolerated.

The government has no right to interfere in the toughest decision a woman will ever make.

First off, murdering your own child should be a tough decision. Imagine how cold-blooded a woman would have to be to say that it was no big deal. However, just because a decision is tough does not mean it is either morally defensible or beyond the scope of the law. If a man is thinking about killing his 10-year-old daughter to collect on an insurance policy, it is logical to assume that it is a tough decision for him to make. But that doesn't mean it should be legal or that it is no one else's business.

The real question is, why is abortion the toughest decision a woman will ever make? The only possible explanation is that buried inside every woman who submits to an abortion is the knowledge that she is murdering her own child.

Any government that can tell a woman she can't have an abortion, can tell her she has to have one.

This question is founded on the bizarre assumption that the government sometimes passes laws and then forces people to participate in the outlawed activity. This is classic abortion industry double-talk. The realities are, (a) there is not one example of the federal government or any state making something illegal and then forcing people to do it, (b) before 1973, when abortion was illegal, neither the federal government nor any state forced women to have abortions and (c) currently, the only women on earth who are being forced to have abortions by their governments live in countries where abortion is legal. The only way the U.S. government would ever be able to force American women to have abortions is for abortion to remain legal.

The government should stay out of abortion altogether. Don't subsidize it with tax money, and don't prohibit it with laws.

That's like saying that if we neither subsidize nor prohibit lynching blacks, we're staying out of racism. That is nonsense. When the government permits something, it is giving it official sanction. In this case, by allowing abortion the government is involved. It is promoting and protecting it.

The government has no right to force a woman to have a child.

Can you imagine a guy who's on trial for murdering his five-year-old using as a defense that the government has no right to tell him he has to have a child? That's exactly what this question suggests. The fact is, legally protecting the lives of unborn babies has absolutely nothing to do with forcing a woman to have a child.

onmessage

Women can decide for themselves whether they want to have a child or not, by choosing not to get pregnant. The pro-life position has never included a mandatory motherhood provision. But medical science makes it clear that once a woman is pregnant she already has a child. Our goal is to see that her baby is given the same right to life as everyone else.

The government should not be involved in the practice of medicine.

First, telling a doctor that he can't intentionally kill someone is not practicing medicine. Second, the government is already heavily involved in the practice of medicine. In fact, medicine is one of the most highly regulated industries in America. The glaring exception is abortion, which is virtually unregulated.

If our state restricts abortion, women will just go to other states.

A state cannot abdicate its responsibilities based on what another state might do. What other states are doing about a particular issue is irrelevant. If one state legalizes cocaine use or incest, does that mean other states should also? Most states have laws against prostitution, but if a man wants the services of a legal prostitute he can go to parts of Nevada. Does that mean other states should legalize prostitution? There is a thriving business in some foreign countries catering to people who want to have sex with children. Since these perverts can get what they want in other countries, does that mean we should make it legal in America? If that's our yardstick, we should do away with our entire legislative process since virtually everything we make illegal is legal somewhere else.

The government has an obligation to fund abortions for poor women.

Just because someone has a right to do something doesn't mean that the government has to pay for it. Americans have the right to buy new cars, but the government has no obligation to buy them for people who cannot afford them. The Second Amendment protects the right to keep and bear arms, but that doesn't mean the government has to provide free guns to poor people. Every citizen is guaranteed the right to free speech, but the government does not buy public address systems or radio stations for poor people so that they can have equal access to the ears of their fellow citizens. We also have freedom of religion, but that does not mean that the government has to purchase Bibles for poor churches.

•••

Abortion advocates say that the real issue is not abortion, but choice. Then they say that the government should take money from people who believe that abortion is murder and use it to pay for someone else's abortion. In other words, the abortion industry demands that women have the choice of killing their children, but even pro-life taxpayers should have no choice about paying for those killings.

The pro-choice crowd tries to defend public funding of abortion by pointing out that a system of government like ours invariably demands taxpayers to pay for things with which they disagree. The most common comparison they make is to military spending. They will point out that people who are opposed to war are forced to pay taxes that are used to fund the military. However, the abortion industry's argument is that the government has no right to be involved in the abortion decision. So the issue here is not whether the government should fund activities which some taxpayers find objectionable, but whether the government should fund activities which the recipients of those funds say is none of the government's business. To understand how ridiculous this is, imagine how much money we would give to a defense contractor who said that the national defense was none of the government's business. Either something is the government's business or it's not. If it's not, then the government has no obligation to pay for it.

•••

Perhaps by refusing to pay for abortions with tax money, we are in effect protecting the children of poor people more than we are the children of rich people. However, if the abortion industry is so committed to the idea of killing the children of poor women, there is a way to solve the whole problem. They claim they are not in the abortion business for profit, but to serve women. If that is true, why couldn't they put a small percentage of the proceeds from every abortion they sell into a fund to pay for abortions for poor women? They could even set this fund up so that people could support it with voluntary contributions. If the abortion industry's rhetoric about this alleged "pro-choice majority" is not a lie, there would be plenty of money to buy poor women all the abortions they want.

I am against abortion, but when I vote I look at all issues. Besides, most elected offices have no impact on abortion.

To be pro-life is to recognize that abortion is the intentional slaughter of children. It is illogical for anyone who holds that view to then say, "Even if a politician approves of butchering children, as long as his position on taxes is right I could support him." The person who says such a thing about taxes—or any other issue—is either lying about being pro-life or doesn't have even a clue what being pro-life actually means. For someone who is truly pro-life, a politician's positions on other issues are irrelevant if he supports the legal killing of children. As for the claim that most elected offices have no impact on abortion, that too is irrelevant. If someone running for office were a member of the Ku Klux Klan, voters would not ignore that fact just because the office he was seeking had no impact on the issue of race. That same dynamic applies to abortion. A person who supports the slaughter of the unborn is not morally qualified to serve in any public office.

Don't get hung up on abortion. Politicians and judges have other issues to deal with and we should not have litmus tests.

First, all issues are not equal. Because abortion takes the life of an innocent human being, then America is participating in the largest holocaust in the history of the world. It is illogical to say that a politician's or a judge's position on that is equivalent to their position on any other issue. Interestingly, the number of people killed during the terrorists attacks on the World Trade Center is virtually the same as the number of unborn children killed every single day in American abortion mills. In short, for the unborn every day is 9/11. If all of us born people were being hit like that, we would not be saying that there are "other issues" to deal with.

As for the suggestion that we should not have litmus tests, that is rubbish. A politician could be attractive, intelligent, experienced and have all the right answers to the important issues of the day, but if he was found to be a member of the Ku Klux Klan his career is over. Make no mistake, in America today Klan membership would be a litmus test. Also, if someone was nominated for the Supreme Court and it was discovered that he had written a law review article saying women should not be allowed to vote, you can bet that would be a litmus test. If a politician said that the terrorists who flew airplanes into the World Trade Center may have had legitimate reasons for doing so, his position on other issues would be irrelevant. The fact is, there are hundreds of litmus tests and any politician who says he doesn't have any is lying. Sadly, even many pro-lifers have bought into this nonsense that abortion shouldn't be a litmus test.

The government has no business telling a woman what she can or can't do with her own body.

To suggest that there is no circumstance in which the government can tell people what they can and cannot do with their own bodies is nonsense. The government routinely enacts laws which prevent people from doing certain things with their bodies. Just to name a few, people are not legally allowed to sell their bodies for sex, or sell organs from their bodies to people who need transplants, or put certain drugs into their bodies.

The most important issue here is that the woman's body is not the only body involved in an abortion. The baby is a separate individual from the mother with its own genetic code, blood type, fingerprints, brain, nervous system and internal organs. About half the time it is even a different sex. The unborn child feels pain independent from the mother, can be awake while she is asleep or asleep when she is awake. The baby can be healthy when the mother is ill or ill when she is healthy.

In fact, it is now fairly routine for children to be operated on before they are born. In 1999, a Tennessee physician had just completed such a procedure and was in the process of closing the incision in the mom's abdomen. Before he could do so however, the child punched his arm through the incision and wrapped his hand around the doctor's finger. Photographer, Michael Clancy was photographing the surgery for *Life* magazine and he immediately snapped a picture which ended up on magazine covers and television sets around the world. The question is, if the unborn is not a separate human being from the mother, who was it that grabbed the doctor's finger? Was it the mom?

Also, it is a biological fact that the unborn child has its own DNA code, its own blood type, its own fingerprints and hair, which any competent forensic expert could easily identify as having come from that child. In other words, if it were possible for an unborn child to commit a crime it has everything necessary for prosecutors to identify it in a court of law. Further, there is no possibility that this identifying evidence could point to the mom. So whether the standard is legal or biological, there is simply no rational way to deny that the unborn child is a separate and unique individual from its mother. So does the government have a legitimate right to ban abortion? The better question is, does any legitimate government have the right to permit such an atrocity?

Abortion is about empowering women and allowing them to make their own choices.

Look at the faces of women entering abortion clinics and see if any of them look empowered. What you'll see is fear, desperation, profound sadness, and resignation. What you will never see is women who feel empowered or in control. The reality is, if you're looking for the weakest, most subservient women in our society, check out the waiting room of the local abortion clinic. Some say "choice" is about letting women control their own bodies, but no group of women has less control over their bodies than those who submit to abortions. You can also be assured that when it's over, not one of them will be proud of what she did. In the final analysis, the decision process for abortion seems eerily similar to the decision to commit suicide. Both are choices made by unhappy people who have been convinced they have no other choice.

The issue is whether we trust women to be their own moral agents and make good moral decisions.

This is no different than someone saying that even though he is opposed to incest, he trusts men to be their own moral agents. Pro-aborts, especially pro-abortion politicians, often resort to this nonsense because they feel incapable of defending the pro-choice position. In their minds, saying that they "trust women" eliminates the need to defend something which they realize is indefensible. Others use it as a way to intimidate pro-lifers into silence by making it appear that anyone who is anti-abortion is anti-woman.

•••

The assertion that being pro-life means you don't trust women is an insult to every pro-life woman. Among the millions of people in the pro-life movement the majority are women, including most of the movement's leaders. To suggest that this predominately female organization seeks to squash other women would be silly if it were not so condescending.

•••

To argue that society should allow people to make all of their own moral decisions sounds good. Unfortunately, it doesn't mesh with human nature. The fact is, societies pass laws based solely on the realization that people can't always be trusted to do what's right. If that were not the case, we wouldn't need laws at all. But in the real world, all human beings—men and women—are capable of making immoral decisions, especially in a time of personal crisis.

Laws are specifically intended to protect other innocent human beings from having those immoral decisions inflicted upon them.

•••

Do these people seriously think that laws have the power to prevent someone from being their own moral agent? There are laws against murder, but that doesn't prevent a serial killer from being his own moral agent. Before abortion was legal, women who wanted abortions were able to circumvent the law. These women were still their own moral agents, they simply chose to engage in an immoral act that happened to be illegal. Today, when a woman has an abortion she is doing something legal, but no less immoral.

The point is, changing the law does not change morality. This "moral agent" nonsense is just a pathetic attempt to make abortion seem morally acceptable. By using the term "moral agent" to describe the woman who pays some degenerate to slaughter her own child, abortion advocates hope to make it appear that she is acting on strong moral convictions. In the final analysis, what abortion defenders want is for abortion to have moral approval. That, they will never get.

•••

No rational person would oppose laws against armed robbery by saying, "We should just trust each individual to make his or her own moral decision about whether stealing is right or wrong." When laws against rape were being enacted, it would have been asinine for someone to suggest that the issue wasn't rape but whether we trust men to make their own moral choices. However, that's no different than saying that the issue isn't abortion but whether we trust women to make their own moral choices.

If we are going to blindly trust women to make morally correct choices about abortion, why not trust them to make morally correct choices about everything? Let each woman make her own moral choice about whether to stop at red lights. Let each woman make her own moral choice about whether to embezzle money from her employer. Let each woman make her own moral choice about writing bad checks. Let each woman be her own moral agent when it comes to drug laws and laws against prostitution. Let each woman business owner be exempt from discrimination laws which make it illegal for her to refuse employment or service to minorities.

Each of these laws prohibit women from making their own moral decisions just as much as laws prohibiting abortion would. In fact, every law on the books prevents women from choosing to engage in a particular activity and says that women can't be trusted to make that decision. So why isn't it the pro-choice position that women should be exempt from all laws? Are they saying that women cannot be trusted to decide whether to sell their bodies for sex or refuse jobs to minorities, but can be trusted about whether to have their own children slaughtered? Do they trust women or don't they?

•••

Let's imagine that a woman has an abortion scheduled for tomorrow, but she gives birth in her home today. If the baby survives, should she be allowed to kill it? The child was going to be killed the next day anyway. Is she only allowed to pay someone else to kill her baby but not allowed to kill it herself? Why should she lose her "right to choose" because of a premature delivery that was totally beyond her control? Are we saying that we trusted her to make the right moral decisions while she was pregnant, but once she gave birth we no longer trusted her? That seems odd since the only thing that happened was that her baby changed locations.

This is a women's issue. Men have no say in whether women have the right to get an abortion.

We are supposed to be beyond the point where people are excluded from decision making based on gender. Also, to say that because of their gender men have no right to be involved is not only sexist, but hypocritical. The pro-choice crowd never tells men who are pro-abortion to stay out. For example, they don't tell the Bill Clintons or John Kerrys of the world to mind their own business. In fact, they invite them to be speakers at their conventions. They have never said that the 1973 Supreme Court had no right to be involved in the *Roe v. Wade* decision in spite of the fact that every single member of that court was male.

They don't appear to have a problem with the fact that the overwhelming majority of abortionists in America are men. They never say anything about the male "escorts" outside the abortion mills. They never even say anything about sexually irresponsible men who coerce, threaten, of force women into abortions. Of course, it is somewhat understandable that they wouldn't have a problem with this last group since that's the backbone of the American abortion industry.

It is pretty clear that the pro-choice movement's message is that there are three groups of acceptable men: those who put women in crisis pregnancy situations, those who build political careers off women in crisis pregnancy situations, and those who make money off women in crisis pregnancy situations. The "bad men" are the ones who think women deserve better than abortion.

•••

People who think men have no right to be involved in the abortion issue should be careful what they ask for. After all, polls consistently find that women oppose abortion at a higher rate than men. Women are also more opposed to government funding of abortion, more active in the pro-life movement, and more likely to favor banning abortion outright. Obviously, if the pro-aborts were to exclude men from the issue, their support would plummet.

•••

If the argument is that men shouldn't be allowed to participate simply because they can't get pregnant, what about women who can't get pregnant? Should only fertile women of childbearing age who are not practicing birth control be allowed to have an opinion about abortion? What about all these older post-menopausal women we see on television shrieking about the right to abortion? Since they can't get pregnant should they be excluded? Or how about lesbians who have no intention of ever getting pregnant, are they told to sit down and keep their mouths shut? Or let's say some pro-abortion activist develops ovarian cancer and requires a hysterectomy. Once she can no longer get pregnant, does she get thrown out of the movement?

•••

If we establish a principle that men have no right to be involved in the abortion issue, what issues are we going to say women have no right to be involved in? The reality is, this whole argument is a fraud. We don't shut people out of issues just because they are not directly affected by them. We don't say white people can't participate in efforts to rid our country of racism, simply because they aren't its victims. We don't say only Jews can speak out about the Nazi holocaust. We don't say that since only men play professional football, women sports reporters are not allowed to cover the NFL. We don't tell young people they have no business trying to stop the abuse of the elderly in nursing homes. We don't say that only children can speak out against child abuse.

It is obnoxious to say that men have no right to speak out against the killing of children. In the first place, men don't need to be given the right to speak out against the killing of children, they already have a responsibility to do so. Real men don't just stand around with their hands in their pockets while helpless babies are slaughtered for money. In fact, any man who is frightened into silence and inaction because of his gender wasn't really much of a man to begin with.

Also, to say that men have no stake in abortion is to ignore the biological reality that every time a woman kills her own child she is also killing a father's child.

If men could get pregnant, abortion would be a sacrament.

Since the beginning of this debate, radical pro-aborts have been regurgitating this nonsense and it is time to set the record straight. If you look at polls taken on the public's attitude about abortion, one thing jumps out. Regardless of whether the poll is paid for by the pro-abortion side or the pro-life side, and regardless of how the questions were slanted to favor one position or the other, one finding almost never changes. With virtually no exceptions, the results show that men are consistently more pro-abortion than women. It seems that men, especially single men, are aware that they are the ones best served and protected by legal abortion.

So while these abortion advocates continue to espouse this "sacrament" garbage, they do so with full knowledge that it's a bald-faced lie. They are fully aware that the data shows that the ability to become pregnant actually makes a person less supportive of abortion. Of course, the abortion lobby finds that fact to be counterproductive, so they just ignore it.

•••

The only people who ever tried to sell the idea that women will never be equal to men unless they can legally butcher their children, are those who have either a financial or political interest in abortion. The average woman, regardless of her views on abortion, is simply not gullible enough to be convinced that protecting the unborn would mean relegating women to the status of nothing more than the property of their husbands.

Let's not forget, with almost no exceptions, pioneers of the women's movement like Susan B. Anthony, Mattie Brinkerhoff, Sarah Norton, Emma Goldman, and Elizabeth Cady Stanton were quite outspoken in their opposition to legal abortion. In fact, Alice Paul, who helped write the original Equal Rights Amendment and worked 50 years for its passage, called abortion, "the ultimate exploitation of women." Even suffragist newspapers like *Woodhull's and Claflin's Weekly*, had editorial policies which openly attacked abortion and abortionists. (For more information on pro-life feminism see: Victoria-Woodhull.com)

These early women's rights advocates correctly saw abortion as patronizing and paternalistic. What they recognized back then remains true today. Abortion doesn't free women, it devalues them. Abortion says they are second-class people whose problems are so trivial they can be handled with a "quick-fix" solution. These women knew that abortion favors sexually predatory and sexually irresponsible males. It allows them to sexually exploit women in a relatively risk-free environment. These guys can have their fun, and if a pregnancy occurs the woman involved can just be "vacuumed out" and used again.

True feminists also know that abortion lets men buy their way out of responsibility. The fact is, no other single factor has freed more sexually predatory and sexually irresponsible men than womens' willingness to submit to abortion. It is, has always been, and will always be, a safety net which makes it easier for women to provide responsibility-free sex to men.

The reality that abortion is a protector of men is now so well known that some abortion advocates no longer even bother to deny it. In fact, some even say it should be celebrated. On May 11, 1990, on the nationally syndicated radio commentary program *Spectrum*, one very vocal proponent of abortion-on-demand, Ann Taylor-Flemming, was expounding on the need for their side to bring more men into the cause. She said this should be done because of the service abortion renders them. This is what she had to say about men, women, and abortion:

> *"I came of age with the women's movement. It has given license to my ambitions and dreams, and filled me with the fervor for equality that permeates all that I do. But this time, I want to turn the tables a bit. Take an issue that always seems like a women's issue and pitch it directly towards the men out there. And that issue is abortion ... it's time now to invite the men of America back in, to ask them to raise their voices for choice ... I dare say that many of them have impregnated women along the way, and then let off the hook in a big, big way—emotionally, economically and every other way—when the women went ahead and had abortions ... the sense of relief for themselves was mixed with sympathy for and gratitude towards those women whose ultimate responsibility it was to relieve them of responsibility by*

having abortions ... it would sure be nice to hear from all those men out there whose lives have been changed, bettered, and substantially eased because they were not forced into unwanted fatherhood."

Even the most bigoted male chauvinist would never suggest that women have a *"responsibility"* to let the men who impregnate them *"off the hook"* by submitting to abortion. And yet, here is that very philosophy being espoused by someone who claims to be an advocate for women.

Statements like these prove that even outspoken advocates of abortion know that by its nature abortion will always be something which allows men to sexually exploit women. The really deplorable part of this is that they have this patronizing attitude toward women while claiming that the only motive they have for being in this battle is to protect women. Maybe that's an example of that old warning to be suspicious of anyone who says they only have your best interests at heart. (A recording of the Taylor-Flemming quote is on file at Life Dynamics.)

Another point is, not only does abortion protect men, it does so without demanding that they face any personal risk. After all, while the baby that's sentenced to death is just as much his as hers, it's only her body which will be invaded to carry out the execution. You can bet that if these guys were the ones who might end up on the abortionist's table, facing unknown emotional and physical risks, they'd suddenly have a different attitude about sex and abortion.

Then there is the argument that a woman sometimes "needs" an abortion because a baby might interfere with her career. However, true feminists do not ask women to change to meet society's needs, but instead work toward a society in which pregnant women, and women with children, are allowed to fully participate just as they are. If the failures of society clash with the biology of women, a feminist would not say that women are the ones who have to change. Simply put, real feminism does not ask women to solve society's problems by killing their children. In fact, powerful women do not kill their children for anyone or for any reason, nor do they believe that women need surgery to be equal to men.

It is interesting to note that anytime a state has tried to enact legislation prohibiting abortions for sex selection, these "protectors of women" are the first ones to fight against it. They do this despite the fact that it's been proven time and again—by people on both sides of this issue—that when a sex selection abortion occurs the overwhelming majority of the time it's a female baby which ends up dead. These people think so little of women that they won't even stop killing those babies whose only sin is that they would one day be women. The pro-choice mob has apparently decided that if our society wants to view being female as a fetal deformity punishable by death, that's okay by them.

The abortion industry wraps feminism around abortion hoping to hide what it really is. Better than anyone else in our society, these people know that abortionists are nothing more than cowardly, cold-blooded, hired serial killers and moral hyenas who prey on women in troubled circumstances. They also know that abortion has the same relationship to women's rights that pornography has. It cheapens, degrades and victimizes them for the benefit of men. For the abortion industry to suggest that having a clean place to kill their babies is the cornerstone of women's equality is a self-serving and vile perversion of the basic values of true feminism. As pro-life feminist Melissa Simmons-Tulin once said:

> "... women will never climb to equality over the dead bodies of their children."

What you and I believe about abortion is not the point.
The issue is, what does the woman believe.

In other words, it doesn't matter whether abortion is actually murder as long as the person who hired the killer thinks it isn't. If that is going to be our yardstick, why do we only apply it to the unborn? Would we say that members of the Ku Klux Klan should be allowed to legally kill black people as long as they sincerely believe that black people are not really human beings?

Women cannot be free unless they have the right to control their own reproductive lives.

First, abortion is not about controlling reproduction. When a woman is pregnant, it is a biological reality that reproduction has already taken place. Abortion is about killing the child that has been produced. Second, what kind of perverted mind sees the right to kill one's own offspring as a symbol of freedom? As pro-life feminist Frederica Mathewes-Green once wrote that women have abortions for the same reason an animal will gnaw off its own leg to get out of a trap. She pointed out that abortion is not a sign that women are free, but proof that they are desperate.

What gives you the right to tell a woman she can't have an abortion?

Absolutely nothing. In a society of laws, no one is allowed to decide what activities others may or may not engage in. As individuals, we have no more right to tell a woman that she can't have an abortion than we have to tell her she can't rob convenience stores. However, it is perfectly appropriate for there to be laws which say she can't do so. And just as our government has the responsibility and the right to prevent armed robbery, it has the responsibility and the right to prevent the killing of innocent human beings. That includes those waiting to be born.

If abortion is made illegal, how do women guard against having their miscarriages investigated by the police? How do they prove they didn't actually have an illegal abortion?

The police do not investigate instances where no one could be charged with a crime. Since no one is arguing that women should be prosecuted for having illegal abortions there is no motive for the police to investigate miscarriages. It is insulting to women to suggest that they are stupid enough to believe that protecting the unborn would place them at risk of having their miscarriages investigated by the police. The abortion industry needs to answer this question: before abortion was legalized in 1973, how often were miscarriages investigated by the authorities and how many women were prosecuted?

Outlawing abortion will impose an unequal burden on poor women. The wealthy will always be able to go to other countries for abortions.

First, it is interesting to note that poor women are rarely the ones agitating for abortion. What they usually ask for is decent housing, better schools and a chance to rise out of poverty. Instead, the pro-choice crowd offers them abortions. It always seems to be rich, white elitists and liberal busybodies who are so concerned about poor women having access to abortion. Perhaps a hidden agenda is at work here.

Second, this issue assumes that we only pass those laws that we know beforehand will be evenly applied across all social and economic situations. That is untrue. Laws against robbery and drugs impact the poor more than the rich but that doesn't keep us from passing and enforcing them. When the drinking age is raised in one state, richer teenagers travel to other states to purchase alcohol. Some laws (insider trading, stock manipulation, tax evasion, etc.) actually impact the rich more than the poor, but we still enforce them. The reality is, if we were to research this issue we would probably find no law is applied evenly across the socio-economic spectrum. However, when a society is considering whether a certain activity should be illegal or not, the primary consideration is not the socio-economic status of the people who might commit it, but the acceptability of the activity itself.

•••

Saying we should not have laws against abortion because rich people have the ability to get them in other countries, is like saying that we should not have laws against drugs because rich people have the ability to get them in other countries. A more legitimate argument is that laws against abortion discriminate in favor of poor children, since the rich can afford to take their children to other countries to be killed. Any way you look at it, when abortion is illegal a child is safer in the womb of a poor woman than a rich one.

•••

This issue subtly suggests that the children of poor people are less entitled to have their lives protected than the children of rich people. It says that the economic status of a family should be what determines whether their children are worthy to be born or not.

Of course, abortion defenders will never agree, but the solution to poverty is not found in killing the children of the poor. We've been doing that since 1973, and our experience proves that it doesn't work. What poor people need is the ability to fully participate in an economic system that gives them the opportunity not to be poor. Killing their children is the solution of "choice" for wealthy elitists.

•••

In America today, there are legal organizations that represent condemned prisoners who claim they were falsely convicted. And there have been numerous instances where these organizations were able to prove that a convict was on death row awaiting execution for a crime he didn't commit. If a study was done proving that most falsely convicted murderers would lead lives of poverty if they were released from death row, does that mean these organizations should butt-out and let the state just go ahead and execute them? If death is preferable to poverty for the unborn, why isn't it preferable for the born?

The Supreme Court said women have a Constitutional right to privacy, and that includes abortion. Why should a fetus have more rights than the woman?

This is the abortion industry's sleazy way of pitting women against their own unborn children. Abortion peddlers realize that if the public can be tricked into believing that there's no way to protect the unborn without trampling on the rights of women, they will tolerate the slaughter of the unborn. After all, they know women have rights, but to them the rights of the unborn are theoretical.

The word "abortion" is not found anywhere in the Constitution. However, in *Roe v. Wade* the Supreme Court said that a woman's Constitutional right to privacy was broad enough to include the right to abortion. Interestingly, the word "privacy" is also not contained in the Constitution. Neither is the theory of life nor the trimester framework invented in *Roe*. The Supreme Court said that a Constitutional right to privacy is found "emanating from a penumbra" of the liberty clause of the Constitution. These verbal gymnastics are a textbook example of "judicial activism" which simply means that the Supreme Court started with the political conclusion they wanted and twisted the Constitution to make it fit.

After he died, the personal notes of Harry Blackmun, the Supreme Court Justice who wrote *Roe v. Wade*, were made public. His description of how this decision was reached forever removed any doubt about whether it was a judicial or a political decision. From his own writings, it is undeniable that Blackmun and the rest of the Supreme Court found a right to abortion because that is what they set out to find. When they discovered that the Constitution contained no mechanism to support their personal political agendas, they simply invented one that would. In short, they manipulated the Constitution to justify what they wanted to do, in the same way some people manipulate Scripture to justify what they want to do.

Having said all that, a sound argument can be made that there is a Constitutional right to privacy. However, it is an established Constitutional principle that rights are not unlimited. For example, libel and slander laws impose a limit on free speech. Even consumer protection laws limit someone's right to free speech by prohibiting merchants from saying anything they want to about their products just to get more customers. The free speech of oil company executives is limited when they are told they can't gather in a private meeting to discuss their pricing structure or they face indictment for price fixing. The fact is that there are many legitimate limits to the right of free speech. We also have a Constitutional right to the free exercise of religion, but that doesn't mean we can kill someone even if we sincerely believe that our faith requires human sacrifice.

The point is that one of the guiding principles the founders used to design our government was that absolute freedom always produces anarchy. They made it clear that every right expressed in the Constitution has legitimate limits. The other thing to remember is that not only are rights limited, they have value relative to each other. For example, a store owner does not have the right to shoot a shoplifter—even if that is the only way he has to recover his property. That is because our society places a higher value on the thief's Constitutional right to life than it does on the store owner's Constitutional right to own property. Clearly, this infringes on the store owner's right to own property, but it is an infringement based on the relativity of rights which the law and the average American accepts as justified.

Regarding privacy, there are many things which occur in private that the law doesn't allow. Before society can say someone's right to participate in a certain activity is derived from his or her right to privacy, it must first answer the question, "The privacy to do what?"

This principle of rights having limits and relativity is how the law weighs one individual's rights against another's. In the case of abortion, the question is not whether a woman has a right to privacy, but whether her right to privacy supercedes her child's right to life. To say that it does is to contend that every right expressed in the Constitution has limits, but that there are no limits to one which is not expressed but had to be found "emanating from a penumbra." Of course, the only legitimate view is that when one individual's "choice" will cost another human being his or her life, that choice cannot be considered a matter of privacy.

●●●

onmessage

To show how far the Supreme Court will go to justify its *Roe v. Wade* decision, in *Planned Parenthood v. Casey*, they upheld abortion's legality on the grounds that it involved, *"...one's own concept of existence, of meaning, of the universe..."*

First, how much credibility should we give a Supreme Court that defends its decisions with this sort of mystical psycho-babble? Also, how far are we willing to go in applying this Supreme Court standard? Satanists, believe that the strong have a right to exploit the weak, and that they must be allowed to practice human sacrifice. Nihilists believe that because nothing has meaning, any act is morally acceptable. There are animal rights activists who consider animals at least as important—if not more important— than people, based on their belief that people harm the earth while animals live in harmony with it. Should they be allowed to kill humans in order to protect animals? Charles Manson believed that people who lived within the confines of ordinary society were "pigs" and should be killed. When his murder conviction was upheld, where was the Supreme Court's respect for his *"concept of existence, of meaning, of the universe?"*

<u>I am not for abortion on demand, I support the compromise reached in *Roe v. Wade*.</u>

This rhetoric is primarily espoused by pro-choice politicians who are trying to keep the abortion lobby satisfied while appearing reasonable to the general public. To accomplish that, they have to conceal from the American people the fact that *Roe v. Wade* actually legalized abortion for all nine months of pregnancy and for any reason whatsoever. For over thirty years, they have been able to carry out this deception because of a scam perpetrated by the Supreme Court in 1973.

Harry Blackmun, the Supreme Court Justice who wrote *Roe v. Wade*, clearly understood that the country would not support abortion on demand. However, his writings prove that this was the political goal he and others on the Court wanted to accomplish. So they devised a scheme to disguise what they were doing. They issued *Roe v. Wade* and included the following language which gives the appearance of allowing states to prohibit abortion after viability:

> *"State regulation protective of fetal life after viability has both logical and biological justifications: and if a state is interested in protecting fetal life after viability, it may proscribe abortion during that period except when it is necessary to preserve the life or health of the mother."*

Roe .v Wade
U.S. Supreme Court
January 22, 1973

Legal decisions such as this normally have a section which defines the important words and terms used in the ruling. An interesting fact about *Roe* is that the Court omitted any definition of the word "health." However, at the exact same moment they issued *Roe*, they also issued what's known as a "companion decision." That's a situation in which the Court issues two or more decisions on a common subject that must be read together in order to get the complete effect of the ruling. The companion decision to *Roe* is called *Doe v. Bolton* and it contains the Court's definition of health:

> *"... in the light of all factors—physical, emotional, psychological, familial, and the woman's age—relevant to the well being of the patient. All these factors may relate to health."*

Doe v. Bolton
U.S. Supreme Court
January 22, 1973

So the court rules that states can prohibit abortion under certain circumstances unless the pregnancy threatens the woman's life or health. This creates the illusion of a compromise. At the same moment, they bury within *Doe* a definition of health so broad that it encompasses any circumstances in which a woman might be

45

pregnant, thus removing all elements of the phony compromise. What made this scam work is the fact that the Court knew that the part of their decision which legalized abortion would be the one receiving all the attention, while the companion to it would be mostly ignored—except by lawyers, judges and state legislatures. And it worked. Most people have heard of *Roe v. Wade* while very few have heard of *Doe v. Bolton*, yet they were equally important.

The result of all this is seen on page three of a report issued in June of 1983 by the United States Senate Judiciary Committee:

> *"The Senate Judiciary Committee observes that no significant legal barrier of any kind whatsoever exists today in the United States for a woman to obtain an abortion during any stage of her pregnancy."*

The bottom line is, there are two things to remember about this situation. First, when you hear a politician say that he or she supports the compromise reached in *Roe*, keep in mind that most politicians are lawyers. That means they studied this in law school and are completely aware of both *Roe* and *Doe*. In other words, they know good and well that no such compromise exists. Second, whenever you see abortion legislation that includes exceptions for the "health" of the woman, this means there are no restrictions of any kind. This is precisely why the abortion lobby always demands a health exception in any abortion-related legislation. They realize that it renders the legislation completely meaningless.

The Supreme Court settled this issue. They said that the fetus is not a person and that abortion is a Constitutional right.

The Supreme Court has a long history of discovering that one of its prior decisions was wrong. In the 1857 *Dred Scott* decision, the Supreme Court ruled that there was a Constitutional right to own slaves. If we are to accept that abortion is a settled issue simply because of a Supreme Court ruling, shouldn't the American people have just accepted that the slavery issue was settled in 1857? There was also a time when the Supreme Court allowed women to be barred from voting. In fact, the law once viewed women as little more than the property of their husbands. Some states even described the methods and reasons men could use to beat their wives. Should we have also accepted those issues as settled?

The Supreme Court's ruling that abortion is Constitutional because the unborn are not "persons" is the same tactic they used to justify slavery. In the *Dred Scott* decision, they ruled that slavery was Constitutional because black people were not "citizens." Clearly, if the Supreme Court can make whole groups of people Constitutionally invisible by simply tossing them into these ambiguous categories, then Constitutional rights mean nothing.

How can a fetus have Constitutional rights before it is viable?

Viability is a false issue for several reasons. First, the two 1973 Supreme Court decisions which legalized abortion said that states could—under certain circumstances—prohibit abortion after viability. However, they then defined those circumstances in such a narrow way that they are effectively non-existent. The result was that abortion became legal right up to the moment of birth with the issue of viability being discarded as irrelevant.

Second, in those rare instances where a state has passed restrictions after viability, it is left to the abortionist who is being paid to kill the child to determine whether it is viable or not. To leave this decision to someone who obviously has a legal, political and financial interest in the outcome is a classic example of letting the fox guard the hen house.

Third, science has now produced proof that human beings are actually viable from the moment of conception. Because of invitro-fertilization, we now know that even at its earliest stages human life is capable of surviving outside the womb if given the proper environment. When a woman's egg is fertilized in a petri dish, that new life is only placed inside the mother because medical science has not yet developed an environment that will substitute for the womb. In other words, viability is a function of medical technology and is wholly unrelated to the question of whether or not the unborn are living human beings. That is further proven by the fact that premature babies are now routinely surviving at gestational ages that would have been unthinkable a hundred years ago, despite the fact that unborn children aren't biologically different than they have ever been.

Fourth, if the issue is that the unborn are not viable because they are dependent upon another individual in order to survive, that does not end at birth. By this standard a two-year-old born baby is no more viable than an unborn baby. Both are dependent on someone else for their survival. In fact, almost every commonly accepted description of viability can be applied to several people who are already born, including the severely handicapped, the senile, the comatose or unconscious, surgery patients under general anesthesia, people with Altzheimers, etc. If the guiding principle to the right to life is the ability to survive without others, do the people described here have a right to life? If so, why does our society apply this viability standard only to the unborn?

How can tissue that is only a quarter of an inch in diameter have Constitutional rights?

In the first place, only a moron could see a sonogram image of an unborn child and dismiss it as mere tissue. Also, the vast majority of abortions happen well past the time when the fetus is that small. In fact, most women don't even know they're pregnant at that point.

Finally, if size is the yardstick for determining Constitutional rights, how big does a human being have to get before it starts having these rights? Is weight or height the primary determining factor? Do rights come on gradually as size increases, and if so what is the ratio of size to rights? Should men have more rights than women since they are generally larger? If someone loses weight do they also lose rights?

onmessage

The Constitution says that only people who are "born or naturalized in the United States" have Constitutional rights. So how does a fetus have Constitutional rights?

It is clear that Constitutional rights are not limited only to those who are born or naturalized in the United States. For example, if a foreign tourist is murdered while in America, the perpetrator will be indicted. Obviously, the law acknowledges the victim's right to life despite the fact that he or she was neither born nor naturalized in the United States.

Laws prohibiting abortion are relatively new. By English Common Law, abortion was even legal when our Constitution was written. Why should we outlaw it now?

Whether abortion was legal or not at that time is debatable, but what possible difference would it make anyway? Over the years, we have passed many laws that didn't exist then and we've eliminated a lot that did. For example, at the time America was founded, it was legal to own slaves and illegal for women to vote. As for abortion, if modern technology and medical science has shown us anything it is the undeniable humanity of the unborn. This is an advantage previous generations simply didn't have.

Why should abortion be outlawed when polls show that the majority of Americans are pro-choice?

The pro-choice position is that abortion should be legal on demand through all nine months of pregnancy, for any reason whatsoever, for no reason whatsoever, paid for with tax dollars and without parental involvement even for minor children. There has never been one poll in even the most liberal state which showed majority support for that position.

The most that can be said is that a majority of people support abortion in the extremely rare "hard-case" situations. Since even abortion industry studies show that almost no abortions are done

49

for these reasons, the only conclusion is that most Americans do not support the overwhelming majority of abortions that are actually performed. This "pro-choice majority" rhetoric has always been a lie and the abortion industry's own actions prove it. Anyone who truly believes that their political viewpoint is shared by the majority of the American people, will fight their battles within the legislatures where the majority prevails. However, the abortion lobby has spent the last thirty years doing whatever it takes to keep the abortion issue out of the legislatures and in the courts. That strategy exposes the fact that their "pro-choice majority" rhetoric is nothing more than political spin.

There is no consensus for making abortion illegal.

So what? In 1850 there was no consensus in America for making slavery illegal. That didn't make slavery morally defensible. At one time there was no consensus for letting women vote. At one time the consensus was that the earth is flat. In fact, history is littered with popularly held beliefs that were later proven wrong. Also, if we are going to say that consensus should drive abortion policy, that becomes just one more reason to overturn the *Roe v. Wade* decision. After all, in 1973 there was absolutely no consensus for legalizing abortion on demand.

Also, courage often means going against popular consensus. Unfortunately, in modern politics that sort of courage is, for all practical purposes, extinct. Today, a politician's positions on issues are usually whatever the polling data tells him they should be. That is why they are called politicians and not statesmen.

If abortion is illegal, what should the penalty be for a woman who has one?

Historically, laws against abortion have only targeted the abortionist. When abortion was illegal before, women were not indicted for having illegal abortions. For several pragmatic reasons, the pro-life movement wants to see that same approach used when abortion is again illegal. First, except in the extremely unlikely event that a woman is actually caught in the act of having an illegal abortion, a conviction would be virtually impossible.

Second, the woman is the best source of information and evidence needed to convict the abortionist. If she faced prosecution, she would never admit to the abortion which means the state would not get the evidence needed to convict the abortionist. That would leave him free to kill again.

This doesn't excuse the woman for having participated in an illegal act. It simply recognizes that the public interest is best served by removing the abortionist from society, and that legal sanctions against the woman would reduce the chances of that happening. It's no different than the authorities granting immunity to a small-time drug user in exchange for information on a big-time drug dealer. Remember, the goal of the pro-life movement is to stop abortion. Imprisoning a woman who had an illegal abortion would prevent nothing since her child is already dead, but imprisoning the abortionist might save thousands of babies in the future. If giving women a pass on prosecution is the only way to get these guys, that is a deal worth making.

Third, given the shortage of jail space in America, it makes no sense to take up a cell with a woman who had an abortion when that same space could confine an abortionist who might do them by the thousands. And make no mistake about it, jail is precisely where these moral degenerates deserve to be. Women who submit to abortions may or may not be fully aware of what they are doing, but the same cannot be said of the abortionist. When they pull those tiny arms and legs and heads out of women, they know for a fact that they are committing the most brutal of murders. There is not one person sitting in a jail cell anywhere in America who's committed an act any worse than an abortion. Furthermore, not one of those people victimized someone as utterly helpless as an unborn baby. So not only are abortionists hired serial-killers, they are cowards as well.

onmessage

The bottom line is that for the pro-life movement there is no practical incentive for jailing women who submit to abortions. If the pro-choice crowd thinks it's unfair or inconsistent for abortionists to go to jail but not their customers, they need to be the ones lobbying for legislation to put women in jail. Just leave us out of it.

How can pro-lifers justify saying abortion should be illegal even when the pregnancy threatens the life of the mother? What about her right to life?

When articulating the pro-life position, the issue which intimidates pro-lifers the most is having to defend the argument that there should not be an exception even when pregnancy threatens the life of the mother. Before one can understand how to defend this view, he or she must fully appreciate why it is absolutely imperative that the pro-life movement never embrace exceptions.

First, when we say that abortion is ever acceptable, we are in effect adopting the pro-choice position. We are saying that, under certain circumstances, it is acceptable to kill a child in order to accomplish a greater good. At that point, the only difference between us and our opponents is the technicality of where the line gets drawn, and nothing makes our argument that it should be drawn in one place any more morally sustainable than their argument that it should be drawn somewhere else.

Even our opponents recognize that this is true. On August 4th, 2004, Planned Parenthood President, Gloria Feldt, was interviewed on KABC radio in Los Angeles, California. During that interview she made the following statement about pro-lifers:

> "... if you press them they will almost always say that they believe in any case that the life of the woman—if a woman's life is at stake—that it should take precedent ... so they're already to some degree pro-choice they just don't know it."

It is appalling to think that this woman—the leader of the most prolific baby killing machine the world has ever known—understands this and so many of our own people don't. (A tape recording of this statement is on file at Life Dynamics.)

Second, some pro-abortion legal scholars have speculated that if the law ever prohibited abortion except to save the life of the mother, such an exception could become a loophole to allow any elective abortion. Their argument is that if a woman claimed she would commit suicide if denied an abortion, that would be enough to satisfy the legal definition of a threat to her life.

Third, when we are able to publically justify that there should not be an exception even when pregnancy threatens the life of the mother, we move the American people past a crucial threshold. When they see that a legitimate argument can be made to prohibit abortion even under this circumstance, it becomes easier for them to understand why there should be no exceptions under any circumstances. After all, this is the "gold-standard" for exceptions.

So how is it defended? To begin with, understand that with modern medicine the chances that continuing a pregnancy to term might kill the mom are extremely rare. However, in those cases where that possibility exists, **the crucial issue is intent**.

If an automobile accident has trapped two passengers in such a way that saving one might take the life of the other, the emergency personnel on the scene would never *intentionally* kill one to get the other one out. Their approach would be to do everything possible to save both and if in that process one loses its life that is a regrettable but allowable outcome. Again, however, the emergency care workers would never take an action that was *specifically intended* to take the life of any of the people involved.

That same dynamic applies when pregnancy threatens the life of the mother. The woman's physician should be directed to do whatever is possible to save both mother and baby. If in that effort the unborn child dies, that should be viewed a regrettable but lawful outcome. But again, no action should ever be legal if its acknowledged intent is to take the life of an innocent human being. The point to remember is that when a woman is pregnant there are two living human beings to consider, and just as it would not be justifiable to intentionally kill the mother to save the baby, it is equally indefensible to intentionally kill the baby to save the mother. Contrary to what abortion apologists claim, the pro-life position is not that the baby's rights are superior to the moms, but that they are equal. This is a perfect illustration of that philosophy.

The bottom line is, the pro-life movement must always defend the pure "no-exceptions" position. However, we are fully capable of articulating that position in a way that protects women without caving in to our opponents' utilitarian and immoral view that it is sometimes necessary to intentionally kill innocent children.

Why should a woman who was the victim of rape or incest have to bear a child?

Abortion for rape and incest victims is a very cynical way to address this issue, and it trivializes the harm that the victim suffered. It is as if someone pats her on the head and says, "Now everything's better. You've had an abortion."

When pregnancy occurs as a result of rape or incest, the baby is indeed the child of the perpetrator. What is often overlooked is that this baby is also the child of the woman. To suggest that inflicting violence on her baby will somehow benefit the mother is cruel to each of them. As a society, we have an obligation to see that every rape or incest victim is offered whatever assistance is needed to put her life back together again.

In recent years, there have been many books, reports, studies, etc., written about this very subject. Some were written by sociologists, some by professional researchers, and others by rape and incest victims. Naturally, this wide range of backgrounds and experiences leads to an equally wide range of suggestions for how to help rape victims cope with the problems they face. However, they almost universally agree what the problems are. They will tell you that these victims feel dirty. They feel helpless, no longer secure in their own homes. Some even experience shame or guilt, as if they were responsible. Often their sense of having been violated fills them with anger and rage toward all men. Many suffer low self-esteem. These are the most common hurdles which experts say rape victims have to overcome. Interestingly, pregnancy is seldom listed.

The reality is, having an abortion at a time when she's not yet over the shock of what's happened to her may actually make it harder to put this episode behind her. There are many examples of women saying that while they will never forget the rape or incest, they have learned to accept and live with it. But among those who had abortions, many say they will never be able to accept the fact that they killed their own baby. Through abortion, these women became not only victims of someone else's violence, but of their own as well. For many, it will be this second act of violence that "re-victimizes" them for the rest of their lives.

On the other hand, you never hear a woman who decided not to have an abortion later say she wished she had. Once she is able to deal with the feelings of shame and guilt, of feeling dirty, the anger, the rage, the feeling of helplessness or low self-esteem, she seldom views the child as another bad thing that happened from the situation, but maybe the only good thing that came out of it. If she keeps the child, that will certainly be the case for her, and if she decides to place the baby for adoption, it will be the case for another family.

Although it is understandable that some rape and incest victims will not see these children as a blessing but a curse, placing the babies for adoption will mean this "curse" will last for a few months. Killing these children could haunt them forever. Regardless of the circumstances, abortion never results in fewer victims but more. So, while the contention that abortion should be allowed for rape and incest victims may be driven by compassion, the reasoning behind it is severely flawed.

Unfortunately, when a sexual predator deprives someone of her right to decide for herself whether to have sex, he takes from her something neither the law, nor society, nor any individual has the power to give back. There is simply no logical basis for believing that allowing a woman to inflict violence upon her own child will lessen the effects of the violence that was done to her or benefit her in any other way.

•••

Every unborn child is a living human being, and that remains true even when a baby is conceived through the most deplorable of circumstances. Further, if the legal protection afforded unborn children can differ based on the circumstances of their conception, there is absolutely nothing which says this discrimination has to end at birth. If an unborn human being conceived through rape or incest is less valuable than one conceived through a loving act of its parents, that same thing is true about a five-year-old. If a drunk driver runs over and kills a child, are we going to give him a lesser sentence if we find out the child was conceived through rape? If a parent kills their two-year-old and their defense is that the child was conceived through rape or incest, are we going to let them off?

The bottom line is, children do not find their right to life in the circumstances of their conception, and it is disgusting that someone would painfully execute a completely innocent baby for a crime that was committed by his or her father.

•••

If the guiding principle for abortion in rape and incest cases is that the woman shouldn't have to have a child that was fathered by a rapist, consider the following scenarios. A married woman discovers that she is pregnant after being raped by a man of another race. She wants the baby if it is her husband's, but not if it was fathered by the rapist. Should she be allowed to wait until the baby is born so she can see what race it is, and then have it killed if it is not her husband's child? Or what if a woman had an ultrasound, was told her baby was a boy, but learned at birth that it was a girl. Should she be allowed to kill the child because she would have aborted it had she known it was a girl?

•••

If the argument for abortion in rape or incest cases is that the cause of the pregnancy was beyond the woman's control, imagine that a woman who was impregnated through rape has an abortion scheduled but she gives birth in the car on the way to the abortion clinic. The pregnancy is far enough along that the baby might survive. Should she be allowed to legally kill the baby there in the car? After all, the circumstances of its birth were no more within her control than were the circumstances of its conception. If we were willing to let her kill her child on the basis that the pregnancy was beyond her control, why would we take that right away because of a second event which was also beyond her control?

How can you tell a woman whose doctor says her fetus is handicapped that she has to have it? Besides, these children can lead terrible lives.

To begin with, doctors can make mistakes. Women often give birth to perfectly health babies despite having been told during their pregnancies that their children had problems. However, the most important thing is that, (a) people with disabilities are not less valuable than those without, and (b) they have the same right to life as anyone else. While someone's life may not be one we would choose for ourselves, that does not give us the right to end their life. No one has the right to decide that another human being's life is not worth protecting, not even the mother.

If we're going to say perfect human life has value but imperfect life doesn't, why does that discrimination have to end at birth? If a drunk driver kills a five-year-old, do we let him off the hook if the child had Down's syndrome but charge him with a crime if the child was healthy? Or what if a father kills his handicapped two-year-old because he decided its life wasn't worth living, do we look the other way? If someone was born perfectly normal and healthy, but later became handicapped, are they now less entitled to the protection of the law than they were before? What about someone who not only has a life that is less than perfect, but is also a financial burden on society? Will we just decide that their life isn't worth living?

The point is that once we start down the path of saying one person can decide whether someone else's life has value, there's no way to say where it ends. Why would one person's standard for making that decision be more valid than another person's standard? If we say that Down's syndrome is handicap enough to justify abortion, what do we say to someone who honestly believes their unborn child's black skin or red hair is a handicap? In other words, exactly what constitutes a handicap? If someone wants to be an opera singer, a squeaky voice is a handicap. If a young lady has her heart set on being a model, being short is a handicap. So where is the line drawn, who draws it and what are the guidelines for deciding where to draw it? Who gets to design the "perfectness" scale?

•••

Why would this "kill-them-for-their-own-good" philosophy have to be limited to the unborn child? If we truly believe that it is compassionate to abort the handicapped in order to spare them the possibility of living a miserable life, surely it would be even more compassionate to kill those people who are already living a miserable life. So why don't we just round up all the non-perfect people in America and execute them like we are currently executing the unborn?

If you think this is preposterous, recall the "Baby Doe" case. In 1984, she was born in Bloomington, Indiana with Down's syndrome. A very common condition with newborns that have this condition is that their esophagus is not attached to their stomach—a problem that is correctable through a relatively simple and highly successful operation. Even though the surgery was necessary for this little girl to survive, her parents refused permission for her to have it, having decided to allow their baby to starve instead of living with Down's syndrome. The physicians involved correctly looked upon the baby as their patient and felt a duty to give whatever life saving

onmessage

assistance was medically required. With the aid of a local pro-life organization, they sought protection in the courts for "Baby Doe."

The battle went from court to court until it reached the Indiana Supreme Court where a judge declared the child a non-person and authorized what he called an "abortion ex-utero" (outside the womb). He ruled that the baby could be starved, but it would have to be given water because dehydration would inflict "unnecessary pain" on the child while the starvation was in process.

Eight days later, Baby Doe starved to death in the hospital where she was born. During the time between when this story became public and the day she finally died, six families asked to adopt her.

For those who think the Baby Doe scenario couldn't become routine, consider the following quotes from people with well documented pro-choice views:

> *"There is little evidence that termination of an infant's life in the first few months following extraction from the womb could be looked upon as murder...It would seem to be more 'inhumane' to kill an adult chimpanzee than a newborn baby, since the chimpanzee has greater mental awareness. Murder cannot logically apply to a life form with less mental awareness than a primate."*
>
> Winston L. Duke
> Article: *The New Biology*
> *Reason* Magazine, August 1972

> *"If a child were not declared alive until three days after birth, then all parents could be allowed the choice that only a few are given under the present system. The doctor could allow the child to die if the parents so chose and save a lot of misery and suffering."*
>
> Dr. James D. Watson
> Nobel Prize winner
> *Time* Magazine, May 28, 1973

59

onmessage

"No newborn infant should be declared human until it has passed certain tests regarding its genetic endowment and if it fails these tests, it forfeits the right to life."

Dr. Francis Crick
Nobel Prize winner
Pacific News Service, January, 1978

"In our book, <u>Should the Baby Live</u>, my colleague Helga Kuhse and I suggested that a period of 28 days after birth might be allowed before an infant is accepted as having the same right to life as others."

Peter Singer
Professor of Bio-Ethics
Princeton University

"It is reasonable to describe infanticide as post-natal abortion ... Infanticide is actually a very humane thing when you are dealing with misbegotten infants. We might have to encourage it under certain conditionalities of excess population especially when you're dealing with defective children."

Joseph Fletcher
Professor of Ethics
Harvard Divinity School
From his article, *Infanticide and the Ethics of Loving Concern*, in the book, <u>Infanticide and the Value of Life</u>, Prometheus Books, 1978

"Infanticide has a logical continuity with abortion and even with contraception."

Edward Pohlman
Researcher, Planned Parenthood
Federation of America, from the book, <u>Psychology of Birth Planning</u>, Shankman Publishing Company, Cambridge MA, 1967

onmessage

Obviously, anytime the subject turns to handicapped people, abortion advocates try to justify what they do by talking about how humane it is to put them out of their misery. In other words, they try to sell the idea that abortion is done in the best interest of the one being killed. But notice that the above quotes primarily focus on what abortion does for others, not for the one being aborted. That fact exposes the very core of pro-abortion mentality. These statements, like others too numerous to list here, prove that the battle over abortion isn't about rights or freedom, it's about selfishness, greed and irresponsibility.

•••

To say that we're going to execute unborn children because of their handicaps, sends a clear message to handicapped people that we think they'd be better off dead than disabled. The revealing thing is that handicapped people don't say this. They know that when you kill handicapped people, you're not saving them from a life of misery you're denying them the only life they have. When the pro-choice mob says "better dead than disabled" what they mean is not that the disabled would be better off dead but that society would be. The handicapped are not executed in order to put them out of their misery, but to put them out of our misery. Like everything else associated with abortion, the guiding principle is selfishness.

•••

How big is the leap between the right to kill an unborn child because of its handicaps and the responsibility to do so? How long until our society says to a woman pregnant with a non-perfect baby that she has an obligation to abort because her child is going to cost the taxpayer more to support than it will ever return to society? And once that's routinely said, how much more time has to pass until people who don't voluntarily meet this responsibility are forced to do so?

For those too naive to think something like this couldn't happen here, during a 1986 symposium entitled, "Prenatal Diagnosis and Its Impact on Society" Dr. James Sorenson, Professor of Socio-Medical Sciences at Boston University stated that, *"American opinion is rapidly moving toward the position where parents who have an*

61

abnormal child may be considered irresponsible." If someone thinks this is farfetched, at one time it would have been farfetched for people to suggest that couples who have large families are irresponsible. Today that is a common attitude.

•••

When a society decides that some human beings have value while others do not, it falls into an abyss with dark and inevitable consequences. Obviously, handicapped people do sometimes have very difficult lives that no one would choose for themselves. But we must remember that the abortion industry's solution is not between a life with handicaps and one without, but between a life with handicaps and death. The decent solution is for our society to do what it can to help the handicapped live as normal a life as is possible. Civilized people do not contend that the way to treat their handicapped citizens is to slaughter them.

As for handicapped children, the fundamental distinction between the pro-life movement and the pro-choice crowd is that we see the handicap as the problem while they see the child as the problem. In short, we don't think being handicapped should be a crime punishable by the death penalty.

No woman ever wanted to have an abortion. They do it because they need to. They have good reasons.

If it's true that no woman ever wanted an abortion, then it is obvious that the most compassionate pro-woman thing would be to help them not have abortions. After all, if a woman was thinking about committing suicide, it would be moronic to say that you helped her out by selling her a pistol. Yet that is precisely what the pro-choice crowd does. The only thing they are willing to do for women in crisis pregnancy situations is to sell them the abortions which they readily admit no woman wants.

Also, if abortion is morally defensible why should the reasons women have them matter? Why should pro-abortion people care if abortion is used frivolously? It shouldn't matter if the woman is aborting because she is a poor, downtrodden mother of seven, suffering from gestational diabetes and pregnant with the severely deformed child of a rapist, or if she is a wealthy conceptual artist who got pregnant on purpose because she wants to use her dead fetus in a sculpture. The fact that abortion advocates go to such great lengths to pretend that women have legitimate reasons to butcher their children, shows that even they know abortion itself is completely indefensible. Remember, doing what is right never has to be justified. The act justifies itself.

How can we tell a woman whose baby is going to die anyway that she can't have an abortion?

First, doctors are not always right when they make this diagnosis. Second, from a moral standpoint there is an enormous distinction between the natural death of a child and the intentional killing of one. It is the same as the distinction between a man dying from a heart attack or being shot and killed in a holdup. Third, if a man is accused of murder and during his trial we discover that the victim already had a fatal disease, do we let the accused go free? Does this "going-to-die-anyway" standard only apply to the unborn?

I think these abortions where the baby is ripped apart are terrible, but I don't have a problem with the abortion pill.

When the Nazis went from shooting their victims to gassing them, it may have been more aesthetically pleasing, but it was certainly no more morally acceptable. Their victims were just as dead.

The same is true about abortion. A doctor may be able to deceive himself that using RU-486 to kill someone is different than slicing them to death, but he's not fooling anyone else. He's like a man who poisoned his wife trying to portray himself as morally superior to the man who bludgeoned his wife with an ax. The fact is, whether an abortionist uses a scalpel to kill his victims or a chemical, he's still a cold-blooded hired serial killer. And given that his victims are totally defenseless children, he's a coward as well.

63

onmessage

NOTE: When the Nazis converted from bullets to gas, the chemical they chose was called Zyklon B. This gas was developed by a company named I.G. Farben. After the war, I.G. Farben changed its name to Hoechst AG in an attempt to disassociate itself from the holocaust. Today, Hoechst is a pharmaceutical giant with subsidiaries all over the world, including the United States. In a chilling irony, one of those subsidiaries is a French company named Roussel Uclaf— the developer of RU-486. In other words, the company that provided Zyklon B for the German holocaust, later provided RU-486 for the American holocaust.

What about a single mom who just can't afford another child?

Poverty is not an excuse for killing your children. To suggest that someone's right to life can be denied them because of the financial status of their parents is disgusting. While few people would excuse a father for killing his five-year-old daughter because he couldn't afford her any longer, that is precisely the philosophy advanced when we say it is acceptable to put an unborn child to death because its mother says she can't afford it. This "pleading poverty" strategy is just another abortion industry smoke screen. Their own statistics prove that almost every abortion they sell is to a woman who simply doesn't want to be pregnant.

Pro-lifers talk about late term abortion as if they are common. Late term abortions are never done unless the woman's life is in danger or the baby is either already dead or couldn't survive anyway.

These claims have been thoroughly exposed as lies several times in the last ten years or so. In one example, George Tiller, the notorious late term abortionist in Wichita, Kansas, was speaking at the National Abortion Federation's 19th Annual Meeting, April 2nd through the 4th, 1995, in New Orleans, Louisiana. The subject was late term abortion and Tiller made the following statement:

"We have some experience with late terminations, about 10,000 patients between 24 and 36 weeks and something like 800 fetal anomalies between 26 and 36 weeks in the past five years."

Listen to what this man is saying. He is admitting to killing 10,000 babies between 24 and 36 weeks in a five year period and over 90% of the babies had no fetal anomalies. Moreover, it is illogical to assume that the remaining 9,200 abortions were performed to protect the lives of the mothers involved since, (a) with today's medical technology it is extraordinarily rare for pregnancy to be life-threatening, and (b) abortions done to protect the lives or health of the mothers are done far earlier in the pregnancies. The fact is, Tiller is openly admitting that the vast majority of the late-term abortions he does are strictly elective. To understand how sickening this is, consider that a 36 week baby is almost full term and that it is not uncommon even for babies born at 24 weeks to survive without major health problems.

The next year, the 20th Annual Meeting of the National Abortion Federation was held from March 31 to April 2, 1996, in San Francisco, California. At this event, Martin Haskell, the Ohio abortionist who invented the D&X (Partial-Birth) abortion procedure made the following statement:

"Two of the criticisms that I've been hearing lately about how our side is structuring its debate is that, one, we seem to be taking a position that—in the case of the D&X—that the fetuses are dead at the beginning of the procedure, which is generally not the case. The second criticism has been that we are really skewing the debate to a very small percentage of women that have fetal anomalies or some other problem that really need the procedure verses the 90% who it's elected, at least through the 20 to 24 week time period, and then as you get on towards 28 weeks it becomes closer to a hundred percent. But these seem to be very uncomfortable issues for people on our side of the debate to deal with."

Haskell is openly criticizing his pro-choice colleagues for lying about, (a) the babies targeted by late term abortions being dead before the procedures start and, (b) the women having these procedures needing them for any kind of health reason. Amazingly, he even admitted that as the abortions got later, the percentage that were "elective" went up, with 28-week and later abortions being virtually 100% elective. This is exactly opposite of what the abortion industry still claims when publically confronted about late abortion. To this day, they still claim that late abortions are never done except when something is wrong with the baby or the mother's life or health is in jeopardy. Of course, these quotes prove they are lying. (The actual recordings of these statements are on file at Life Dynamics.)

If abortion is outlawed women will again be forced to back-alley butchers and they will lose their lives.

For more than 30 years, the abortion industry has been claiming that somewhere between 5,000 and 10,000 American women used to die every year from illegal abortions. One pro-abortion lawyer, Frank Susman, was even quoted in a Missouri newspaper saying that in the years immediately prior to *Roe v. Wade*, 30% of all hospital emergency room admissions were for women who had been injured during illegal abortions.

To see how truly outrageous these sort of claims are, look at the total number of American women who died in the years leading up to the legalization of abortion. Statistics published in August of 2004 by the United States Census Bureau show that, annually, slightly more than 50,000 women of childbearing age died from all causes. This number has to be almost perfect since the only women who would not be counted are those who died without anyone ever knowing about it.

Therefore, for the abortion industry's claim that between 5,000 and 10,000 women died every year from botched abortions to be true, we have to blindly accept that between 10% and 20% of all

American women who died before 1973 were killed by illegal abortions. It stretches the imagination to believe that anyone is gullible enough or stupid enough to believe a lie of that proportion. Obviously, the abortion industry concocted these statistics in order to frighten people into supporting their agenda. The fact is, every study ever conducted on the subject of "back-alley abortions" proves that they were extremely rare. Even materials published by pro-abortion organizations show that the overwhelming majority of illegal abortions were performed by licensed doctors who were simply breaking the law.

For example, figures released in 1986 by the Alan Guttmacher Institute (the research arm of Planned Parenthood) show that in the 15 years leading up to the legalization of abortion, the average number of women dying from illegal abortion in the entire United States was 136 per year. For at least three reasons, logic suggests that these figures were probably pretty accurate. First, when a woman died from a botched abortion the cause of death would have been easily identified during the ensuing autopsy. Second, the death would have been officially recorded by an emergency room physician or a medical examiner with no personal interest in the cause of death and no reason to falsify the death certificate. Third, these deaths were always reported to the Bureau of Vital Statistics at the U.S. Public Health Department.

So while the figures might not be perfect, neither can they be off by very much. For the abortion industry to claim that in 1972 as many as 10,000 women died from illegal abortions, but the government was only aware of about a hundred of them, is preposterous. The fact is, almost every researcher who has ever studied this issue— even those who openly support legal abortion—have concluded that, (a) deaths and injuries due to illegal abortion have been grossly exaggerated and, (b) the perception that back-alley, coat-hanger abortions were common is a myth.

•••

Abortion defenders say that if abortion is made illegal, the pro-lifers will be responsible for those women who might be injured or killed during an illegal abortion. The question is, why should we be held responsible for the women the pro-choice crowd is threatening to kill? Think about it. It's pro-choicers who do abortions not pro-lifers. Every single woman who dies during an abortion—be it legal or illegal—is killed by a pro-choicer.

So again, why should we be held responsible for that? Our contact with women facing unplanned pregnancies comes when they seek help from one of our crisis pregnancy centers, and those women don't end up being killed by the people who work there. That only happens to pregnant women who seek the services of pro-choicers, not pro-lifers.

Now if the abortion industry is so concerned about women being injured or killed during illegal abortions, there is a two-part fail-safe plan to address this problem. First, we get everyone on both sides of this issue to sign a statement agreeing that they will never perform an illegal abortion. Second, both sides agree to lobby for legislation requiring that, (a) people who commit illegal abortions must be prosecuted under the same statutes that apply to any other hired killer and, (b) anyone who coerces a woman to have an illegal abortion or helps to arrange an illegal abortion is to be charged as an accessory to homicide. These two initiatives would solve the "back-alley abortion" problem instantly and both ideas would be strongly supported by the pro-life community. In short, we will agree not to do any illegal abortions and to support legislation that would vigorously prosecute anyone who does.

Now, once the pro-choice mob does the same, this problem is over. However, until that time comes, the pro-life movement is through being vilified for what these people are threatening to do to pregnant women. No longer will we allow them to use their coat-hangers to extort us. From now on, every time one of these radical pro-choice fanatics screams about women dying from illegal abortions, we will be there to point out that this blood is on their hands not ours. It is simply undeniable that whenever a mom and her baby are killed during an abortion—both were killed by someone who is pro-choice. Apparently, the real pro-choice position is, "If you don't let us kill helpless babies then we're going to kill pregnant women—but we're killing somebody."

•••

If the motivation for legalized abortion is saving the lives of women, why don't we also legalize rape? After all, we know that sometimes a woman is killed by a rapist only because he wants to keep her from identifying him to the police. Making rape legal would save women's lives by taking away the motivation for killing them. We could also establish rape "clinics" where perpetrators could take their victims to be raped. These centers could offer clean rooms, condom machines, emergency contraception, and perhaps even doctors on staff for those times where a rapist might injure his victim. We might even consider issuing licenses to rapists which require them to undergo routine testing for AIDS and other sexually transmitted diseases.

Obviously, this is a ridiculous proposal, but remember, the pro-choice argument is that, (a) women are going to have abortions regardless of what the law says and, (b) that keeping abortion legal will make sure they take place in a cleaner and safer environment than the back alley. Both of those dynamics also apply to rape. Making rape illegal has not prevented women from being raped, so why not at least try to prevent back-alley rapes? Any way you look at it, if the goal is to save women's lives, legalized rape makes just as much sense as legalized abortion.

> **NOTE:** For a gritty behind-the-scenes tour of the American abortion industry, including a look at the harm abortion does to women, read **Lime 5** available from Life Dynamics.

You people talk about the dangers of abortion, but abortion is safer than childbirth.

To begin with, abortion is certainly not safer for the baby. If there was a way to interview them, they would most likely tell us they'd rather take their chances in a delivery room than an abortion chamber. As for the baby's mother, modern medical technology means that only an infinitesimally small percentage of childbirths have even the potential to cause either maternal death or a serious health problem for the mother. Also, it is now possible for physicians to identify and deal with those extraordinarily rare instances long before the birth occurs.

However, if our country is going to buy into this myth that abortion is safer than childbirth, and if our overriding goal is to protect women, then it only makes sense to encourage women to abort all of their pregnancies. Obviously, that would save the most women's lives possible. Of course, if we want to carry this to its logical conclusion, then we also need to start allowing people to kill their born children as well. After all, children don't just pose a risk to their mothers before birth, they can pose one afterward. Sometimes they cause the death of a parent through an accident, and a small number of children will grow up to one day abuse or even murder their parents. So obviously, we could spare the lives of those mothers by simply allowing them to kill even their born children.

I am opposed to abortion, but I don't believe I have the right to inflict my personal beliefs on others.

You will sometimes hear this stated by members of the general public, but it is more commonly said by politicians who are trying to "finesse" the abortion issue. The trick is to appear philosophically pro-life so they don't have to defend abortion, and functionally pro-choice so they don't energize the abortion lobby. They think this is a sophisticated view, when in reality it is just a cowardly one.

Understand that the only logical basis for someone to be personally opposed to abortion is because they believe it to be the killing of an innocent human being. While claiming to believe that however, they say it should be legal. So what they are really saying is, "Abortion is the intentional killing of a helpless child but I wouldn't do anything to stop it. I am willing to look the other way while someone else takes the life of a child."

onmessage

That is a smoke screen. Only a coward would contend that unborn children are living human beings but that it is none of his business if someone wants to butcher them. It is no different than saying that they are opposed to rape but it is none of their business if men want to rape, or that rape is not an area in which the government should be involved. If the intentional killing of children is not an area of legitimate government interest, then the government has no legitimate interest. Before we support politicians who take this view, we need to ask ourselves what the consequences will be for a country that elects leaders who say they wouldn't do anything to stop what they admit is the murder of children.

Also, are the people who make this statement as tolerant on other issues? Surely, they are also opposed to holding up convenience stores, running red lights, and wife-beating. Do they balk at imposing their beliefs on others regarding these issues? Would they take this position on abortion if they were in the baby's shoes? If someone was about to slice them up with a knife, would they object to politicians stepping in to impose their beliefs on the killer? Probably not. The point is, for those who are already born it is easy to take this "government shouldn't be involved" attitude about abortion. For the born, abortion poses no risk.

•••

For people who say they are personally opposed to abortion but wouldn't outlaw it, the question is, "Besides the unborn, what other category of innocent human beings do you think it should be legal to kill? Are the unborn the only ones?" They also need to tell us if there is anything else they think is wrong but are not willing to deal with as a wrong.

•••

Regarding the statement that politicians don't feel it's their place to inflict their views on other people, why are they running for public office? What do they think their job is once elected? Inflicting their views on others is precisely what legislators are elected to do and every vote they make does exactly that. Further, if a politician is not going to be guided by his own personal views, why tell us what his personal views are during the election campaign? And if he is not going to be guided by his own personal views, whose personal views is he going to be guided by? Clearly, this whole line of reasoning is a fraud.

•••

As for politicians who claim to be Christians but say they won't impose their beliefs on others, that is rubbish. Any Christian who honestly believes that holding public office might place them in a situation where their political duties would conflict with their Christian faith would not seek that office. Imagine that someone claims to be a Christian and says he was raised in the church and loves the Lord. When asked what he does for a living he says that he owns a chain of triple-X theaters and porn shops. He then claims to reconcile this inconsistency by keeping his professional life and his spiritual life separate. Would anyone really believe that this guy is sincere about Christianity?

The same standard applies to politicians. When John Kerry ran for president in 2004, he said his Catholic faith guides all that he does and made him who he is. He also said that he believes that life does indeed begin at conception, but that he would not let his personal views affect the decisions he would make in office. Kerry was lying. A person of true Christian faith would never say that when their faith collides with their political ambitions it is their faith which they will abandon. When a person says they have one set of Christian beliefs but an opposite set of political beliefs, what they are really saying is that God can't trust them. They are admitting that when God wants one thing and man wants another, they will serve man. Perhaps the real question for the rest of us is: if God can't trust them, should we?

The answer to abortion is not in making it against the law but in changing hearts.

The answer to all of humanity's problems is in changing hearts. In fact, we wouldn't need any laws if everyone would always do what is right instead of what is wrong. But until that day comes, we have to have laws. We must remember that the role of the law is not to change hearts but to restrain the heartless. As Martin Luther King once pointed out, the law could not make people love him but it could keep people from lynching him.

In America today, hired serial killers are butchering innocent and defenseless children by the millions. They are the heartless who must be restrained. Our government has no right to allow victims to be murdered waiting for the murderers to have a change of heart. In the real world, most people who commit evil will never have a change of heart and their innocent victims are entitled to legal protection. The bottom line is, if abortion is not murder, why do we need this change of heart? If it is murder, why do we allow the heartless to do it?

You cannot legislate morality.

It is revealing that we always hear this tiring, "you can't legislate morality" argument from people who want society to accept something which they know any decent society finds immoral.

To say that laws can't make an immoral person moral is correct. To say that we don't legislate morality is nonsense. Every law is someone's idea of what is right or wrong. For example, people who are opposed to rape are willing to impose their morality on rapists. They don't care why rapists rape, or what the rapists' moral and religious views are, or whether rapists think women are fully persons. Rape is evil and when people want to do evil it is right for the government to impose its morality on them.

•••

Could any logical person possibly believe that the people who founded this country thought its laws should be made completely free of moral considerations? If laws shouldn't be based on morality, what should they be based on? The reality is that the law is simply society's collective moral values. It is the way society decides which activities it will and will not tolerate. When John Kennedy was running for president, he said that the passage of civil rights legislation was one of his top priorities because, in his own words, it was the morally correct thing to do. He clearly understood that the only legitimate reason for passing any legislation is to achieve a moral objective.

You have no right to tell others what to believe.

The argument that the pro-life movement is trying to tell people what to believe is absurd. Laws are not passed to control thought but to control behavior. When society passes laws against armed robberies, the law doesn't care what someone thinks about armed robbery as long as they don't commit them. For the pro-life movement, that dynamic also applies to the unborn. We don't care what people think about them as long as they don't kill them.

What gives you people the right to force your religious beliefs on others?

A person does not have to be especially religious to say it's wrong to murder a child, any more than they have to be religious to say it's wrong to steal money. It's just that there are certain activities civilized people won't accept regardless of their religious beliefs or even if they don't have any.

Abortion is one of those issues. In reality, abortion is a civil rights and a human rights issue. Just because so many people in our movement are personally motivated by their religious beliefs does not make abortion a religious issue. If the argument is that abortion should be off limits to the law on the basis that most pro-life people are Christians, then it is only logical to do away with laws against armed robbery since one of the Ten Commandments is, "Thou shalt not steal." In fact, if we are going to reject a law simply because it is supported by religion, and since there is hardly anything illegal which is not also prohibited by Scripture, then obviously we have to do away with all of our laws. Let's also not forget that the civil rights movement was dominated by pastors and that it was often headquartered in churches. That didn't make civil rights a religious issue.

onmessage

Can someone be pro-choice and a Christian?

In a word, no. Included in Christian theology is the belief that God is the author of life and that He is incapable of making mistakes. Elective abortion openly denies both of those. If God is the author of life, and if He does not make mistakes, from a Christian perspective the only logical conclusion is that when life exists in the womb it is God's will that it be there. People who claim to be Christians, while saying that men should be allowed to legally take that helpless and innocent child's life, are either self-delusional or outright frauds. In short, given that "choice" now means the killing of children, there is no more legitimacy to Christians who call themselves pro-choice than there is legitimacy to Christians who might call themselves pro-adultery or pro-armed robbery.

During His ministry, Jesus never spoke out against abortion.

First, given that not every word Jesus uttered is recorded in Scripture, we don't really know whether Jesus ever addressed abortion or not. Second, would the people who make this statement have defended slavery by saying that Jesus never spoke out against it?

The Bible does not condemn abortion.

It is likely that the vast majority of the behaviors which are illegal in America today are not specifically condemned in the Bible. The Bible doesn't even mention insider stock manipulation or child pornography, but it is safe to conclude that Scriptural prohibitions against theft and lust apply.

Moreover, it is a lie to suggest that the Bible is neutral on abortion. It repeatedly warns against doing harm to children, shedding innocent blood, committing murder, etc. Also, in both the Old and New Testaments, there is never a distinction drawn between born and unborn people, nor is there any difference in the language used to describe them. A good example of this is seen in Luke 1:41.

onmessage

In the original Greek, the unborn John the Baptist is called a "brephos" which means "babe" or "baby." In the very next chapter, the born Jesus is also called a "brephos." Also, when Scripture tells us that Elizabeth's baby lept in her womb upon being in the presence of Mary, are we to conclude that this makes no statement about the status of the unborn? If so, and if the Bible is silent on abortion, then it is also logical to conclude that Scripture would be unconcerned about whether these women would have aborted Jesus and John the Baptist. After all, by pro-choice reasoning, at this point they didn't exist.

The bottom line is, it should not be lost on us that throughout the Bible and in both original languages, the unborn is always referred to in exactly the same manner as the born. Logically, there is no alternative but to see this as evidence that God views them as the same and, therefore, intends them to be treated the same.

NOTE: Scriptures relating to the unborn child include:

Genesis 25:22-24	Job 31:15	Psalm 22:9-10
Psalm 139:13-16	Jeremiah 1:5	Hosea 12:2-3
Luke 1:15	Luke 1:41	Exodus 21:22-24

<u>As a Christian, I know that abortion is wrong, but I don't feel that the Lord is leading me to take a stand on this issue.</u>

Imagine that a group of men are standing outside their church on a Sunday morning when they see that a screaming young girl is being raped and murdered in a field next to the church. When the police arrive they ask these men what they did when they saw what was happening. They reply, "Well, we gathered together and prayed for her and we also prayed for the rapist to have a change of heart. But, you know, we're Christians and we didn't feel led by the Lord to actually do anything to stop it."

Who on earth is going to be stupid enough to buy that nonsense? Everyone would instantly know that these guys didn't get involved because they were more concerned for themselves than they were for the girl.

•••

In March of 1964, a young New York City woman named Kitty Genovese was brutally raped and murdered while dozens of nearby people looked on. Later, New York police interviewed 38 of these people and asked them why they ignored her cries for help. Most answered they just did not want to get involved, that it was none of their business. Today, this same ugly scenario is repeated over 3,000 times every day. That is the number of children being butchered in American death camps while the church looks the other way, does not get involved, and soothes its conscience by claiming it is none of its business.

What we are seeing is something that previous generations have also experienced. Whether it was slavery 200 years ago, the Nazi holocaust 70 years ago or abortion right now, church leaders seldom have the courage to do the right thing in terrible times. Most will either choose the wrong side or sit silently on the sidelines and let the evil go unchallenged. The fact is, America is in a state of moral meltdown solely because the church has traded its moral authority for comfort and popularity. We are to the point where if you show Americans a plastic garbage bag full of aborted babies, many will be far more concerned about whether the plastic bag is going to be recycled than about the babies inside.

The reason abortionists can go on killing is due to the silence of the churches. Every time a pro-lifer puts tithes or offerings into the collection plate of a cowardly church that won't take a stand against abortion, he is in effect giving money directly to the pro-life movement's biggest enemy. The irony is that we refuse to support politicians who abandon the unborn, and we refuse to give our money to businesses that support Planned Parenthood, yet at the same time we freely give our money and support to pastors who support abortion with their deafening silence. Somewhere along the way, we apparently concluded that church leaders should be held to a lower standard than our plumbers and politicians.

77

onmessage

<u>As a Christian, I know abortion is wrong, but God gave us free will. It is not our place to judge a woman who wants to have an abortion.</u>

First, we are not judging women who submit to abortions, we are trying to stop them. Second, would this be your attitude if they intended to kill your children rather than their own? Or what about some man who is on trial for killing his wife? Would you say we have no right to judge him? In other words, does this "free will" standard apply across the board or only when the victim is waiting to be born?

It is interesting how "open-minded" people can become about murder once they figure out that they cannot be the one who is murdered. In fact, the single biggest factor in the battle over legalized abortion is that the people who defend it are already born. You can be assured that if they could all be transported back to the womb, their views on "choice" and "free-will" would be considerably and immediately different.

<u>Abortion is just one of many issues the church has to be concerned about. The economy, the homeless, the death penalty, U.S. military policy, education, health care, and hunger are important too.</u>

Sometimes called the "Seamless Garment" or the "Consistent Ethic of Life," this philosophy is generally advanced by two groups of people. The first group is closet pro-aborts, or abortion agnostics, who want to avoid revealing their positions on abortion. The other group consists of luke-warm pro-lifers who are looking for some way to justify their own—or their church's—inaction on abortion.

By equating abortion with other social ills, both groups are attempting to neutralize the abortion issue and silence pro-lifers. This argument is also commonly used by people who call themselves Christians but want to justify voting for a pro-abortion politician. To expose what a scam this really is, just ask one of these people if they would ever vote for a white supremacist on the basis that race is just "one of many issues."

Obviously, there is no denying that America faces many societal problems. However, if abortion is the taking of a human life—and even many pro-aborts are now openly admitting that it is—then our country is engaged in the largest holocaust in world history. To suggest that the wholesale slaughter of 45 million children—a number which increases by more than 3,000 each day—is even in the same universe as tax policy, or homelessness, or poverty, or any other issue is indefensible. For someone who claims to be a Christian to make such a statement is pornographic.

Of course, if the people who take this approach were the ones who might be sliced open alive and have their heads crushed, it's pretty certain they would suddenly stop saying that abortion is just "one of many issues."

I know abortion is evil, but my obligation is to save souls, not bodies. Besides, those babies go to heaven anyway.

This is a shabby excuse used by some Christians, mainly preachers, to justify their appalling inaction over abortion. The question is whether the preacher who says this applies it to anyone other than the unborn?

If he saw that his own daughter was about to be murdered, would he try to stop it or just shrug it off because she is going to go to heaven anyway? If he was on a jury hearing a murder case in which the evidence makes it absolutely certain that the accused is guilty, but the victim's pastor convinced him that the victim went to heaven, would he let the killer go free? If an ax murderer came into the sanctuary and started hacking at people he knew to be saved, would he just look on with a smile, pleased to know that all of these people were going straight to heaven? In fact, any pastor who was sincere about this philosophy would practice it himself by immediately drowning everyone he baptizes. That way he could make certain they go to heaven by eliminating the possibility they might reject God later in life.

Obviously, these hypothetical scenarios are preposterous, but they are certainly no more preposterous than trying to excuse the murder of children on the basis that they are sinless.

When a woman miscarries, are you saying that God did something evil? Is God an abortionist?

First, God is incapable of doing anything evil. Second, there are many things which God is allowed to do which man is not allowed to do. In fact, the inability (or the refusal) to accept that reality is at the heart of the pro-choice mentality. Third, to suggest that a naturally occurring miscarriage is the same as an elective abortion is obscene. If a 60-year-old man dies of a heart attack, from a moral perspective that is quite different than if he had been shot to death by a carjacker. That is the exact distinction between natural miscarriage and induced abortion.

I believe that abortion is wrong, but I also believe that the solution is prayer.

Statements like this demonstrate a complete ignorance about both belief and prayer. First, belief is irrelevant if it does not control behavior. A rapist might believe that what he is doing is wrong, but that means nothing to his victim. Most people who engage in adultery probably believe that adultery is immoral, but that is meaningless if they continue to do it. By the same token, a little girl who is being ripped apart by some abortionist gains little comfort from people thinking that what she is going through is wrong.

Second, prayer is not intended to be a substitute for action but an addition to it. If a child is hit by a car and possibly dying in the street, any rational person would call an ambulance and try to summon the best possible emergency care. Prayer would certainly be an invaluable part of that process, but not even the most sincere

Christian would suggest that prayer is the only thing that should be done for this child.

So the question becomes, if we believe that the unborn has the same right to life as the born, why are we so willing to say that all we will do to save the unborn is pray for them? When we take that position, we are in effect adopting the pro-abortion mentality that born children and unborn children can be treated differently.

If a woman just isn't ready for a baby, maybe it's best that she terminate the pregnancy and ask God to bring the child back at a better time.

First, when a woman is pregnant it doesn't matter whether she is ready for a baby or not. She has a baby. The only thing left to decide is whether she is going to kill it, keep it, or place it for adoption. Second, abortion is not the termination of a pregnancy it is the termination of a human life. All pregnancies terminate, the only question is whether they terminate with a live baby or a dead one. Third, when a baby is killed it cannot be brought back at a "better time." The mom may have another baby later in her life, but the baby she aborts is dead forever. Finally, don't for a moment think that God is going to conspire with a woman to butcher the baby which He gave to her.

Since even theologians can't agree when life begins or when the soul enters the body, why should abortion be illegal?

Theologians are free to think whatever they want to, but they don't make law. America is not a theocracy, but a republic. As such, it is governed by people we elect to make our laws based on solid physical, scientific, and biological evidence. That evidence makes it clear that abortion kills the smallest, most vulnerable, and most defenseless human being in our community. That is something civilized societies do not allow. Just because some theologians may be a little bewildered about that is irrelevant.

Further, if the standard is that we can kill the unborn because we don't know whether the soul has entered the body, that could also be said about a fully-grown adult woman. We can't legally or scientifically prove that a soul even exists much less prove that one has entered her body. However, that is irrelevant to the question of whether she has a right to life.

No one can prove when life begins. It is up to the woman to decide based on her own beliefs.

No modern medical, scientific or biology text says that life begins at any time other than conception. Simple deductive reasoning also proves that life begins at conception, since that is the only time it can begin. In the continuum between conception and death, any point other than conception is strictly arbitrary.

Also, if we don't know when life begins then we don't know if it has begun at birth, or at age five, or at 50. So how can we go into court and convict someone for murdering a 50-year-old when we don't know for sure that the victim's life has even begun?

That is obviously a ridiculous position, but no more so than saying we can slaughter the unborn because we don't know if their lives have begun. The biological reality is, if their lives have not begun there is nothing for the abortionist to kill.

•••

Even if it were true that no one can say for certain when life begins, that is not an argument which supports legalized abortion. Imagine that the judge in a murder case said, "We really can't say for certain that the accused is guilty, but we are going to give him the death penalty anyway." No rational person would buy into that. Our attitude would be that before we take this person's life we better be sure we're not taking the life of an innocent human being. So why don't we apply that standard to the unborn? After all, to say that no one knows when life begins is, at the very least, a recognition that it might begin at conception. Shouldn't we stop killing them until we are sure?

onmessage

As for allowing the woman to decide when the life of her child has begun, since when is one person's right to legal protection based on what somebody else thinks about him or her? To see how ludicrous this is, think about two children who are conceived at the same moment. Three months later, one mother talks about her baby, knows its sex, has named it, and has even seen it on an ultrasound screen. The other mother believes that the life of her child hasn't begun yet and decides to have an abortion. The pro-choice mentality is that both mothers are right, despite the fact that it is a physical impossibility for that to be the case. By any scientific, biological or theological standard, it is not possible for one baby to be a living human being and the other one not.

Also, if women are to be the ones who decide when life begins, why should they lose that right by giving birth? Let's say a woman sincerely believes that life doesn't begin until speech is possible. If she kills her three-month-old daughter should she be tried for murder? Did she take a life? Other people believe that personhood is measured by the ability to use tools because that is what separates us from animals. Should a woman who honestly believes that be tried for murder if she killed her child before he learned how to use a can opener? Did she take a life?

A "yes" answer to either of these scenarios destroys the philosophy that women should be allowed to decide when life begins. What makes the decision that life begins at speech or the use of tools, less sustainable than any other arbitrarily decided point? After all, there's no physical or scientific evidence supporting either position. So what gives society the right to tell these women they are wrong, while saying that women are the ones who decide when life begins?

We don't deny that the fetus is potential human life, but that is different from an actual human being.

Only through mind-numbing stupidity could someone suggest that when male and female human beings reproduce they produce something that is only "potential human life." In the first place, if the word "potential" is suggesting that the unborn is only potentially alive, that is demonstrably untrue. Sonograms on women who are even in the earliest stages of pregnancy show movements and heartbeats that do not belong to the woman. Clearly, whatever else the fetus is, no one can logically deny that it is, at least, alive.

Therefore, "potential" must refer to the word "human." However, for that to be accurate, the fetus would have to have the potential of becoming either a human being or some other life form. Perhaps a parrot or a spider. The problem is that there is no record of a human female ever having given birth to anything other than another human being. So while it may be reasonable to say that a fetus is a potential major league baseball star or a potential school teacher, it is laughable to say that it is a potential human being. The biological reality is that the fetus is a living human being because that is the only thing it can be.

Pro-lifers talk about abortion as killing a baby. That is not true. There is a fetus, but no baby.

The word "fetus" simply describes a stage of human development based solely on location. When it moves from inside to outside the womb, it will be instantly described by other names such as newborn or infant, despite the biological fact that it is fundamentally unchanged from when it was inside the womb. As time goes on it will become known as a toddler, a child, an adolescent, an adult, etc. However, at no stage is it any more or less a human being.

Also, if the issue is "development," remember that all human beings develop for their entire lives. A fetus is less developed than a newborn just as a child is less developed than an adult. But being less developed than an adult does not mean that a child is any less a human being. Biologically, the same is true for a fetus.

•••

onmessage

The rhetoric of the pro-choice mob exposes their hypocrisy on this issue. When they are talking about an unborn child they don't intend to kill, they don't say, "How is the product of conception doing?" or "I felt my fetus move yesterday." or "The potential life has the hiccups." If they intend to let it live, they use the dreaded four-letter word "baby." Only when they intend to kill it do they call it something else.

•••

If there is no baby before birth, when a doctor first hands a mom her newborn child, where did it come from? After all, nothing is created at birth. Obviously, something came out of the uterus during the birthing process. Was it some sort of primordial glop that mystically transformed into a baby simply by passing through the birth canal? Isn't it odd that these ever so sophisticated abortion-rights advocates are the only people over the age of 12 who don't know where babies come from? Perhaps they could figure it out by asking a woman who just suffered a miscarriage exactly what it was that she lost.

•••

Pro-lifers aren't the only ones who know that it is a baby that's killed in an abortion. At a National Abortion Federation conference held from September 18th through the 20th, 1994, in Philadelphia, Pennsylvania, Texas abortion clinic director, Charlotte Taft stated:

> *"There was an activist, the same woman that Janie Bush was talking about who—who is a pro-choice activist in the Dallas community. When she came into our clinic—we were inviting her to learn more about abortions—this is a quote from this woman. She said, 'If I believed that abortion was the deliberate ending of a potential human life, I could not be pro-choice.' I said, 'It would be best for you not to see a sonogram.'"*

Less than two years later, at another National Abortion Federation conference held in San Francisco, California, from March 31 through April 2, 1996, New York abortion clinic director Merle Hoffman made the following statement:

onmessage

"...I mean, we are talking about an abortion here. And uh, also that the staff is uncomfortable when a patient said, 'I think I'm killing my baby.' So I'm comfortable with saying, 'Yes, you are, and how do you feel about that?' You know-- 'Oh, you are. You're killing life. You're killing potential life.' I mean, my God, if you don't do that, in nine months you do have a live baby."

Obviously, as these statements prove, these people know exactly what they're doing. It is simply not conceivable for them to pull those tiny little arms and legs and lifeless bodies out of women without knowing that they're killing children. Unfortunately, they just don't care. (The actual recordings of the quotes given above are on file at Life Dynamics.)

Pro-lifers say adoption is the answer, but what about all the black babies that aren't getting adopted right now?

First, this suggests that there are orphanages all over America teaming with black babies whom no one wants. Anyone who knows the first thing about adoption knows that this is not the case. Second, in those rare instances where this problem may exist, the solution is not to kill black babies but to make it easier for them to be adopted. The problem is an adoption system that makes it so expensive to adopt a child that many black families cannot afford it. The other issue is that some regulations make it virtually impossible, for black babies to be placed with non-black families.

A *Wall Street Journal* article published on February 27, 1987, addressed the issue of the bureaucratic barriers to black adoption pointing out that, "... the real villain is the snarl of red tape and tangle of rules, regulations and adoption procedures that screen out prospective black families and inhibit the adoption of wanted children. Those who dominate the selection and placement process often apply inappropriate standards in evaluating the qualifications of blacks to care for their own and other children." The same article quoted statistics from the National Urban League's

Black Pulse Survey which showed 15% of all black households to be "very interested" in adopting a black baby, but the expense prevented them from doing so.

It is offensive to suggest that black families won't adopt as often as white ones. The reality is, most people—regardless of their race—couldn't adopt their own children if to do so meant they had to endure the same process as those who are trying to adopt one who has no home. Today, America's adoption and foster care system is in desperate need of a top-to-bottom overhaul. It is costing the taxpayers billions, depriving good parents of children, and doing irreparable harm to kids who have to grow up without a family.

What about all the children who get adopted by people who abuse or neglect them?

Only the pro-choice mob could seriously expect to sell this loopy idea that it is common for people to spend thousands of dollars, endure a grueling adoption process and sometimes wait for years, just for the purpose of having a child they can sexually abuse, torture, abandon, neglect or kill. Even in those incredibly rare cases where abuse or neglect does occur, it stretches the imagination to believe that the adopted child would say that they wish their birth mother had just killed them. No matter how bad an adoption situation might be, it can't even approach the horror of being sliced apart by some abortionist. If there was a way to interview unborn children, you can bet that every single one would say that they'd rather take their chances in the worst adoptive family than in the best abortion clinic.

When abortion defenders say that because there's this infinitesimally small chance that some adoptive parents may abuse the children they adopt, the best thing to do is just kill the children first, maybe it's just the abortion industry's version of the death penalty. Apparently, they are suggesting that society should avoid the possibility that a crime may take place sometime in the future by simply executing its potential victim today.

onmessage

Let's make one thing clear. The pro-choice solution to the incredibly rare bad adoption is not a good adoption, but an abortion. As is always the case, the only solution these people see to any social problem is baby killing. In this case, their solution to adoption problems is to butcher the adoptees. That's no different than saying we should shoot women to keep them from getting raped. Apparently, defending abortion does some weird things to a person's capacity for rational thought.

Adoption is not the solution. Thousands of children are waiting to be adopted right now. If a baby is not a white, healthy, newborn it stands little chance of being adopted.

The National Counsel for Adoption says that while there is indeed a long waiting list for healthy white babies, there are also parents available for minority and physically challenged babies. They also say that almost half of all adoptions in the U.S. are of special needs children, and their statistics show that the number of adoptions of these children is rising. This is confirmed by Christian Homes and Special Kids, a non-profit organization founded in 1990 to support families with special-needs children. Today, they report that almost half of the families in their network are families in which their special-needs child was adopted. They also report that at any given time they have a database of several hundred families waiting to adopt children with even the most severe physical challenges, including children whose physical problems are known to be fatal.

The truth is, the chances of a newborn baby not being adopted are actually quite small—regardless of circumstances. The problem in adoption is not babies, but older children who come into the adoption system long after their birth. That means that the pool of children currently available for adoption has nothing to do with abortion since these children are already born.

Also, the large number of children abortion defenders claim are available for adoption is based on the total number of children in foster care. They want people to assume that every child in foster care is legally adoptable when the truth is that only a small percentage of them are. And again, since these children are already born, this has nothing to do with abortion. When the abortion industry tries to justify killing children by saying there are children who aren't getting adopted right now, they're talking about two separate and unrelated groups of children. The interesting thing is that the children they want to kill are the ones who are the easiest to place for adoption and, therefore, not part of the problem. The pro-choice position is, "We have a group of children over here (older, already born children) who are difficult to place for adoption, so let's to kill this other group over here (unborn babies) who are very easy to place."

Obviously, the whole argument is absurd. How is a 12-year-old girl who needs a home helped by killing an unborn baby? What that 12-year-old needs is policies designed to make children like her more attractive to adopt. Killing a totally unrelated group of children who aren't hard to place won't help her a bit. Pro-aborts often counter that if the people who want to adopt babies couldn't do so, they might adopt these older children. It would be hard to imagine a more repugnant form of extortion than that. What they're really saying is, "In order to make adoptive parents take the older children we think they should adopt, we'll slaughter the babies they want to adopt." Few statements speak better to their moral bankruptcy than that one. (For additional information on special-needs adoption go online to CHASK.org.)

There are more abortions every year than there are people waiting to adopt. What do we do with all those children after these people have gotten the baby they want?

First, this assumes that once abortion is illegal every woman who would have had an abortion will now place her baby for adoption. There is nothing to support that contention. Actually, before abortion became legal relatively few women with unplanned pregnancies placed their babies for adoption. America's pre-1973 experience proves that unplanned (or even unwanted)

pregnancies do not necessarily produce unwanted children. At the moment a new mother sees her baby for the first time, even the most unwanted pregnancy usually turns into a very wanted baby.

Questions like this also assume that all the people currently on waiting lists to adopt would only adopt one child. The reality is that the vast majority would adopt more than one if it were possible to do so. Right now they don't because very few can afford to. But if the supply of available babies went up, the cost of adoption would go down, and most of these people would jump at the chance to adopt more than one child. These sort of questions also suggest that the number of people wanting to adopt will remain constant. That is untrue. Today, if a family is upper middle class or wealthy, adoption is a possibility but for the typical American family with an average income it's not. That severely limits the number of people expressing an interest in adoption. However, an increased supply of babies would lower the cost of adoption and substantially increase the number of people having the ability to adopt.

Another factor which will continue to increase the pool of parents available to adopt is that the number of couples who are unable to conceive is steadily growing. Already experts are saying that about one couple in six will experience such problems. They say one apparent cause of this is that women are waiting later in life to start their family, which leads to fertility problems. Since this is a trend that is not likely to reverse itself, it will continue to be a substantial factor in the growing number of people who want to adopt. Also, there is less stigma attached to single parent adoption and this will continue to increase the number of people wanting to adopt.

What about a woman who says she could not handle carrying a child for nine months and then giving it up for adoption?

Are we honestly expected to believe that a woman who is not emotionally capable of placing her baby in a good home is emotionally comfortable killing it? To see how truly insane this is, imagine that the police are called to the home of a woman who has slit the throat of her five-year-old son. Her defense is that she killed him because she couldn't afford to feed him any longer but couldn't deal with the heartache of giving him up for adoption. Everyone would know that this woman is either thoroughly evil or criminally insane.

Defending abortion with this excuse is like a man who tells the police that he beat his estranged wife to death because, "If I can't have her, nobody can." When this happens, no one sees this as justification for what he did. This guy is on his way to prison, perhaps even death row. That's because society expects men to have the emotional strength to deal with the pain of knowing that the woman they feel so bonded to is with someone else. We expect them to accept that they don't own their wives or girlfriends, even if they feel like they do. But according to abortion enthusiasts, women are too hysterical and weak for us to expect them to live up to that standard. For them, the behavior they would find reprehensible and criminal in men, is just a "choice" for women.

What about the emotional damage done to women who give up their babies for adoption?

It is only natural that some birth mothers will wonder about, or even experience grief over, a child they placed for adoption. However, it really stretches the imagination to think that the kind of woman who would be subject to these feelings would feel better knowing she killed her baby. What's interesting is, the abortion lobby that pushes this idea that women risk being irreparably traumatized by placing babies for adoption, are the same people who become absolutely hysterical if someone suggests that even one woman was ever traumatized for having her baby butchered.

Why don't you pro-lifers do something to help people who are already born, like the homeless?

There are approximately 3,000 crisis pregnancy centers in the United States funded and staffed almost entirely by pro-life people.

Each provides some or all of the following: counseling about birth control, counseling about abortion alternatives, information about what government help is available, pre-natal care, sonograms, room and board during and after pregnancy, clothing, baby items, medical services, assistance for other children, assistance with adoption, post-natal instruction, help for moms to continue their education, post-abortion counseling, legal counsel and many other services—all of which are provided free of charge to women with unplanned pregnancies.

On the other hand, the abortion industry has raked in billions off of American women by contending that their only interest is in supporting women in problem pregnancy situations. However, if a pregnant woman comes into one of their abortion mills needing help, the only "choice" she is offered is an abortion—provided she has money to pay for it. The fact is, not one of America's 3,000 crisis pregnancy centers is funded or operated by the pro-choice crowd, and when pro-life groups try to solicit money to fund these centers our biggest problem is that almost every pro-lifer we approach is also contributing to other organizations whose sole purpose is to help people.

Obviously, the pro-life movement would like to be able to help more people. Unfortunately, right now we're maxed out just trying to keep the pro-choice mob from butchering every baby they can get their hands on. However, let's say for a moment that no pro-lifer anywhere in the country was involved in one single effort to help anybody. What does that have to do with our opposition to abortion? Where is it written that when someone tries to prevent the slaughter of an innocent human being, that they suddenly become responsible for solving all the world's social problems?

Consider these legal organizations like Innocence Project which represent prisoners who claim they were falsely convicted. These groups have been successful in numerous instances where they were able to prove that a convict was sitting on death row awaiting execution for a murder he didn't commit. The question is, when one of these groups is trying to save the life of someone they believe to be innocent, should they be told to butt-out unless they are doing something about homelessness, and poverty, and all the world's other social problems? Would anyone suggest that unless they are doing something about these issues they have no right to prevent the execution of innocent people?

Obviously, no one would say such an asinine thing. But that is precisely what the abortion lobby says about the pro-life movement. As bizarre as it sounds, their contention is that unless we solve all the world's social problems, then the unborn has no right to life and we have no right to act on their behalf. It appears that defending the slaughter of children does some really strange things to a person's capacity for logical thought.

•••

As for the homeless, the pro-life movement has limited resources and when the choice is between helping people who don't have a place to live or helping people who are being butchered by the millions, we have to choose the latter. However, if the pro-choice crowd is so concerned about homelessness, there is a way they can end it anytime they want to. For years, their chant has been that if pro-lifers are so concerned for the unborn we should be willing to adopt them. We agree. In fact, there are many pro-lifers standing in line right now for the privilege of adopting a baby. So if they'll stop butchering them, we'll take them off their hands.

Now, given that the pro-choice crowd is so committed to the idea of adoption, and since they're so concerned about homelessness, here's a chance for them to put their money where their mouths are. There are far more abortion advocates in America than there are homeless people. So all that needs to happen is for each of them to go down to the local mission or skid row, pick out one homeless person and take him home. Most pro-choice people probably have a spare room he can live in and some extra food in the house. They may even have a car he can borrow to look for a job. In any event, this plan ends the homeless problem instantly, without controversy and without tax money. This same strategy could also be used to eliminate hunger, poverty, unemployment, and any number of other social problems.

Of course, the pro-choice crowd is never going to do this. They are ever so quick to tell the lie that people who oppose abortion don't care about these other issues, but the bigger lie is that they do care about them. The fact is, they've never had any interest in the homeless, or the poor, or the unemployed, or those who are hungry. They simply exploit them as a smoke-screen to keep from having to talk about abortion. They know legal abortion is impossible to defend and these issues are just skirts for them to hide behind.

The world has a major problem with overpopulation. So how would we feed these children when millions are already starving?

The philosophy that it's acceptable to kill certain completely innocent human beings in order to accomplish social objectives is not only the very definition of evil, it is irrational and ineffective. In this case, we're talking about America where millions are not starving. Of the more than 3,000 American children slaughtered every day by abortion, the percentage who would have one day lived in hunger is tiny. For all practical purposes, the number who would have some day starved to death is zero. To kill our children by the millions in order to keep a tiny fraction of them from being hungry is lunacy.

Second, the children who are starving are almost exclusively in third-world nations where repressive regimes often deliberately starve their own people. What kind of sense does it make to try to correct this situation through abortion in the United States? Does anyone seriously believe that the solution to children starving in Ethiopia is more abortions in America?

It is a well-proven fact that people do not starve because of overpopulation or because there is not enough food in the world. The earth produces more food than is required to feed its inhabitants. People starve because of corrupt political systems and poor distribution which denies them access to food. Killing American children won't solve those problems. It won't overthrow a totalitarian regime, won't allow free enterprise in other countries, won't improve farming techniques, won't build roads, won't improve the food distribution system. In fact, we could kill every unborn child in America and it would not provide one single bite of food for one starving third-world child.

•••

If killing people is our solution to hunger, why pick on the unborn? That's an irrational solution to the problem since they are not eating yet, and even once they're born they won't eat much for a long time. If we're serious about using bloodshed to solve hunger, we should be killing adults since they eat more than anyone else. In fact, if we would simply execute everyone who is hungry we could immediately eliminate the hunger problem altogether.

We could also save some food by establishing a pre-set age at which we feel the elderly take more calories out of the food chain than the amount of good they do for society. When someone reaches that age, we would simply "put them down" and save the food they would have eaten for ourselves. Given that abortion clinics are already set-up for this sort of thing, expanding their services to include the elderly would be easy and highly profitable. Also, the government would probably be willing to pay for it with tax dollars since killing these folks would be considerably cheaper than keeping them on Medicare and Social Security.

If we put our minds to it, we could also solve a lot of other problems by implementing this "death-as-a-solution" philosophy. For example, if we made all crimes punishable by the death penalty we would not only help end hunger but we would also lower the crime rate, reduce courtroom overcrowding, eliminate prison overpopulation, lower tax rates, reduce unemployment and end homelessness. Of course, these proposals are ridiculous, but they are certainly no more ridiculous than this idea that killing the unborn is a legitimate way to address world hunger.

As for overpopulation, it is highly debatable whether it is a problem or not. Some new data suggests that a bigger problem is declining birth rates which do not even replace existing populations. But, if overpopulation really is a problem, why limit our options to only killing the unborn? Why not put a legal limit on life at the other end as well? This could be enforced through mandatory euthanasia at a pre-determined age. At the very least, we should immediately outlaw any medical research that's intended to extend life. If overpopulation is a problem, it makes no sense to spend billions of dollars looking for ways to make people live longer.

In fact, whether it's research prohibitions or mandatory euthanasia, bumping off the elderly makes more sense than killing the unborn. The elderly use up more of the earth's resources and the drain they put on our health care system is overwhelming. With our population growing older, and the baby-boomers getting ready to retire, this plan could be exactly what we need to save Medicare and Social Security.

As a taxpayer, I'd rather pay $300 for a welfare mom's abortion than pay thousands of dollars to raise her kid for 18 years.

Arguments like this prove just how sick and morally bankrupt the pro-choice mentality really is. Imagine that a welfare mom's two-year-old daughter fell into an abandoned well. Local authorities calculate that since a funeral is cheaper than a rescue, and since this little girl might well be a welfare recipient for the rest of her life, the financially wise thing to do is just fill the well up with water. Once she has drowned she'd float to the top, the coroner could scoop up the body and bury it, and the taxpayers will have saved a bundle. That sounds monstrous because it is monstrous. But it is no different than saying to poor women that if they will agree to kill their children to save the rest of us money, we'll hire the killer.

•••

If the argument is that executing a child is cheaper than supporting a child, that seems undeniably true. The question is whether we have reached the point where that is the decision we want to make.

If we have, and if we are really serious about saving tax money, let's allow women on welfare to kill their born children. Remember, the guiding principle here is not morality but saving tax money. If we are willing to ignore the biological fact that unborn children are living human beings, why shouldn't we be willing to ignore the biological fact that born children are also living human beings? Don't forget, the only goal here is to save money.

I don't want to pay for all the social problems created by people having children they don't want and can't afford.

The pro-choice crowd has had over 30 years to weed out all the "unwanted people," and no one can argue that they've been stingy in carrying out the death sentences. So far, they've killed over 40 million babies and they continue to kill them at the rate of 3,000 a day. Meanwhile, we are asked to ignore the fact that America has experienced more teenage pregnancies, more hunger, more welfare, more divorces, more women and children living in poverty, more child abuse, more spousal abuse, more deadbeat dads, more gangs, more drugs, more sexually transmitted diseases, more high school drop-outs, more homelessness, and the list goes on and on.

The fact is, every social problem which the pro-choice mob says will get worse if we make abortion illegal, actually became worse after we made abortion legal. Also, the financial burden on taxpayers to pay for these social problems is at record levels and rising. Like it or not, the American taxpayer is subsidizing the abortion industry.

So, where is the payoff we were assured would come from sacrificing our children? Did we kill the wrong babies? Or maybe we haven't killed enough of them yet. Who knows? We've gone this far, maybe killing a few million more would do the trick. So why give up now?

Of course, the answer is obvious. Killing people to solve social problems is not only morally indefensible, it doesn't work. It is also the ultimate act of selfishness. After all, no one ever volunteers to give their own life to solve a social problem, they only insist that others do.

The other question is, even if it did work do we really want to be the kind of country that uses child sacrifice as a tool for social engineering? Can we justify butchering babies who are not even born yet in order to solve problems we created? Can a civilized society afford to view results as if they occur in a moral vacuum? Let's say for a moment that instead of getting worse our social problems had been helped by killing these babies. Would that justify it? Are we prepared to say that the wholesale slaughter of innocent children is acceptable if it profits us?

If that is going to be our attitude, why kill the unborn? They're not part of any of our social problems. If death is an acceptable way to solve social problems, the most efficient way to obtain the desired result is to kill the people with the problem. To end poverty, kill the poor. To end homelessness, kill the homeless. To solve prison overcrowding, execute all prisoners. To solve unemployment, kill everyone without a job. To solve child abuse, kill all abused children, and so on.

Obviously, these are unconscionable solutions to these problems, but certainly no more unconscionable than saying we are going to solve social problems by killing the one category of human beings who had nothing to do with creating the problems and whose death would have no impact on solving them. Another question is, where does a society draw the line when it says innocent children can be killed to accomplish social objectives? The issue is not whether abortion has the ability to accomplish social objectives, but whether it is a morally acceptable way to accomplish them.

•••

If the justification for abortion is to see that every child is wanted, here is a suggestion. We should create a national computer database of people who want to adopt a baby. Any pregnant woman who doesn't want her baby would have access to this database. If there is a person who wants to adopt her baby, she could not have an abortion. If there was no one willing to take her baby, she could legally have the child killed.

Of course, the abortion industry is never going to take this deal because they know there is no such thing as an unwanted baby. Every single baby they butcher is wanted by someone. Their "every child a wanted child" rhetoric is a scam and they know it. They also know that this adoption database would literally put every abortion mill in America out of business overnight. The "disease of unwantedness" was conjured up by these people to justify abortion and create a market for their product.

Some children lead terrible lives. Wouldn't abortion be better than that?

First, if that's going to be our standard, there are a lot of born children already living those terrible lives. Why don't we kill them? After all, if it is compassionate to kill someone who might live a terrible life someday in the future, surely it is even more compassionate to kill someone who is living a terrible life right now. Second, how do we identify which unborn children will lead these terrible lives? Should only women who promise to give their children terrible lives be allowed to have abortions? Also, how can we make sure that we don't butcher some babies who would have had good lives?

Apparently, the argument here is that we are doing these abortions out of compassion. If that's really our goal, shouldn't we first do a national survey of all the people who have lived what we might classify as terrible lives and see what percentage of them would have rather been ripped to shreds in their mothers' wombs? Wouldn't they know better than us whether this is really compassionate or not?

Also, if through some macabre twist of logic it can be argued that abortions benefit those being aborted, could we justify slavery in the same way? Could we argue that a man is better off being a well-cared-for slave in America, than he is starving to death in some filthy AIDS infested third-world country where he has little hope for a better life? If the yardstick is a purely utilitarian one with no moral component, this makes perfect sense. You can also bet that during slavery some slave traders tried that very argument, just as abortion traders try it today.

What about all the children who will be abused because they were unwanted? We need to make sure that every child is a wanted child.

There are some really unusual views on the death penalty out there, but the most bizarre has to be this suggestion that we eliminate child abuse which might occur sometime in the future by executing the potential victims today. That makes about as much sense as trying to eradicate wife-beating by killing all married women or trying to wipe out police brutality by allowing cops to shoot suspects on sight.

Of course, this question completely ignores the fact that abortion is itself the ultimate example of child abuse. The question also assumes that unwanted pregnancies always produce unwanted children. The reality is, even among women whose pregnancies were the most unwanted, it is rare for them to say they don't want their baby. Furthermore, there is not one shred of evidence showing that unplanned or even unwanted children are any more likely to be abused than planned or wanted ones. To the contrary, in 1980 Professor Edward Lenoski at the University of Southern California studied over 600 cases of child abuse. He found that in over 90% of these cases, the parents said that the child they abused had been a wanted child.

Additionally, since abortion was made legal in 1973, we have killed unborn children by the tens of millions yet child abuse has increased dramatically. According to The U.S. Department of Health, Education and Welfare, in 1973 there were 167,000 cases of child abuse reported in the United States. In 2002, the U.S.

onmessage

Department of Health and Human Services reported 1,694,756 child abuse investigations in the United States. Of those, 450,817 were substantiated and another 58,964 were considered to be instances in which abuse was "indicated."

Could this 10-fold increase in child abuse be due to better reporting? Some of it could, but it could in no way completely account for an increase of this magnitude. There is no other rational conclusion but that our country has suffered a staggering increase in child abuse since we legalized abortion.

When you confront abortion defenders with this, they will say there is no evidence that this increase was related to abortion. So to recap, (a) in the 1960s and 1970s the pro-choice position was that legalizing abortion would lower child abuse, (b) America legalized abortion, (c) during the next 30 years child abuse skyrocketed, and (d) the new and improved pro-choice position is that there is no relationship between child abuse and abortion but making abortion illegal will cause an increase in child abuse.

Needless to say, watching the pro-choice gang tie itself in knots trying to justify abortion is seldom boring. Of course, they can never answer two simple questions. First, if legal abortion reduces child abuse by making sure that every child is a wanted child, given that we've executed over 40 million children so far—where did all of the children who are being abused today come from? Second, how many millions more do we have to butcher before this scheme starts to work?

Why should a woman who is acting responsibly and using birth control be subjected to forced motherhood just because her birth control failed?

It is a fact that birth control can fail. However, if we are going to take the position that women should not be forced to take on the responsibilities of having a child simply because their birth control failed, do we extend this same offer to men? If a man was "acting responsibly" by using a condom and his partner was "acting responsibly" by using birth control pills, why should she be the only one who's allowed to avoid responsibility if a pregnancy results?

The point is, it is clear that the pro-choice crowd believes that women should be insulated from "forced motherhood" even after conception. After all, that is what abortion does. They also claim that abortion is an issue of equal rights for both men and women. Therefore, the question becomes, do men have the right to be insulated from "forced fatherhood" even after conception? If a man offers to pay for an abortion, should we say he has fulfilled his legal obligations? This question is especially relevant given that when a woman is pregnant the father of the child has no legal rights. If she decides to abort, he is legally irrelevant and powerless to stop the killing of his own child. If she doesn't abort, he is legally forced to be responsible for supporting the child to adulthood. The question is, how does that reconcile with the claim that abortion is about equal rights? How can "forced motherhood" be wrong if "forced fatherhood" is right?

•••

This idea that when someone is acting responsibly they should be immune from consequences is nonsense. Even when people are acting responsibly while driving their cars, they are still responsible for the damage they might do. The same thing is true about sexual activity. Acting responsibly goes beyond simply taking steps to avoid pregnancy. It is also accepting—before getting sexually involved—that a child may be conceived. While for some people it may seem like a tragedy when birth control fails and a child is created, the far bigger tragedy is when a child is butchered so that its mom and dad can avoid responsibility for their actions.

The best way to prevent abortion is by promoting contraception.

While on the surface this premise only seems logical, in practice it has been proven incorrect. It is widely known that the availability of contraception increases sexual activity—especially among teenagers—at a far greater rate than it increases the use of contraception. That guarantees higher pregnancy rates. Contraception pushers belittle this analysis, yet they offer no lucid alternative explanation why America's dramatic increase in contraception use starting in the sixties was accompanied by a equally dramatic increase in unplanned pregnancies, abortion and sexually transmitted diseases.

Interestingly, this trend continued without interruption until recently when the government began diverting funds from programs that push contraception to those that push abstinence. Now, government statistics are showing that the rates of unplanned pregnancies, abortion and sexually transmitted diseases are declining for the first time in over 30 years.

Despite this, the abortion lobby and the pill pushers continue to market contraception as the holy grail of pregnancy prevention. In private however, they sing a different song. While they will freely lie to the American people, it seems that they are reluctant to lie to each other. In just one example, while citing a study conducted at Cornell and the University of Pennsylvania, a participant in a forum on contraception at a National Abortion Federation event made the following statement:

> "... half of the women put on Norplant, and half put on oral contraceptives—now listen to these numbers—at the end of 15 months, all these women not wanting to become pregnant, 38 percent of the Pill patients were pregnant! Thirty-eight percent! What are we doing? **_We're giving them a fertility pill!_** (audience chuckles). Of the women started on combined oral contraceptives—where we always say point one is the failure rate, one in a thousand—at the end of 15 months, 38 percent were pregnant and only 33 percent were continuing to use Pills. So, when I said to you earlier, 'Well I'd like to see teenagers given condoms and spermicide,' I know what some of you are thinking. You're thinking, 'Ah, Hatcher--come off it! They're never going to

continue to use condoms and a spermicide.' Well they don't continue to use Pills either."

Robert Hatcher, M.D.
National Abortion Federation
19th Annual Meeting, April 2-4, 1995
New Orleans, Louisiana

NOTE: Hatcher is a widely recognized expert in the field of contraception, a professor of Obstetrics and Gynecology, and an author of the book, Contraception Technology.

Another example that the abortion lobby tells one story in public and a different one when they think no one is listening, was seen at a 1994 National Abortion Federation function. A professor at the University of Cincinnati and an expert on contraception, Paula Hillard, presented a talk in which she cited a study that had been conducted regarding contraception use and abortion. In this study, over one-fourth of women having abortions were taking birth control pills. She pointed out that many women—especially adolescents—get pregnant because they don't take their pills every day. In fact, according to the study, more than half didn't do so, with teenagers missing an average of three times a month. Another attendee then commented on her speech:

"...the overview that Paula did was fabulous because it really talks to us about a lot of the issues that happen before and after abortion. I think the most wonderful piece of information was to see that it--it's--the kind of information we need to show to people that women do not use abortion as a birth control method. Because they're all contracepting somehow before in the month that they got pregnant."

Suzanne Poppema, Abortionist
National Abortion Federation
18th Annual Meeting, April 24-26, 1994
Cincinnati, Ohio

onmessage

Amazing as it is, this woman is actually saying that because many women who have abortions were using contraception, that proves women don't use abortion as contraception. In fact, it proves just the opposite. According to the study cited, women are indeed using abortion as secondary birth control which is exactly what the pro-life movement has been saying since day one. Believe me, this woman would never make such a statement in public, nor would she ever say that her abortion customers were *"all contracepting"* when they got pregnant. (A tape recording of both the Hatcher and Poppema quotes are on file at Life Dynamics.)

The important fact is that Hatcher's and Hillard's observations are by no means uncommon. Neither are they new. After a 1958 Planned Parenthood conference, a report was published on its findings which included the following statement:

> *"It was recognized by the Conference participants that no scientific evidence has been developed to support the claim that increased availability of contraceptive services will clearly result in a decreased illegal abortion rate."*

This report was edited by Dr. Mary Calderone, Medical Director of Planned Parenthood. Also, the Chairman of the Statement Committee was Alan Guttmacher for whom Planned Parenthood's research branch is named. (As stated, the above quote specifically refers to illegal abortion. However, that is irrelevant in this context since the question of how contraception use affects pregnancy rates is not influenced by the legal status of abortion.)

One of the participants in this conference was Dr. Alfred Kinsey. When another of the attendees continued to push contraception as a way to eradicate abortion, he responded by saying:

> *"At the risk of being repetitious, I would remind the group that we have found the highest frequency of induced abortion in the group which, in general, most frequently uses contraceptives."*

Clearly, despite their contemporary profit-motivated rhetoric, our opponents have always known that contraception use does not decrease either pregnancy rates or the incidence of abortion. In fact, they have always known just the opposite.

The other problem with this "contraception is a cure for abortion" argument is that many common methods of contraception are, in reality, abortions.

When a woman's egg is fertilized, a new human life is created. Within 24 hours, cell division begins and a few days later this tiny human being will have traveled to its mother's womb and attached itself there. This new life is first called a zygote, then a blastocyst, an embryo, a fetus, an infant, a child, an adolescent, an adult, etc. These labels identify the various stages of human development, but no stage is any more or any less human than the others.

Anything which prevents this process from beginning could accurately be described as contraception. However, once fertilization has occurred, the only thing that can stop the process is death. Manufacturers of birth control pills, birth control patches, birth control injections, morning after pills, etc., say that their products are intended to prevent conception but they readily admit that when this process fails these drugs can also prevent implantation. In those instances, that means they did not prevent the pregnancy from occurring but from continuing. By definition, that is abortion not contraception. Moreover, even though they are marketed as contraception or birth control, intro-uterine devices (IUDs) are specifically designed only to prevent implantation. Again, that is abortion not contraception.

In an effort to hide this from American women, the abortion lobby uses the concocted term "pre-embryo" to describe the stage of human life from fertilization to implantation. They also claim that until implantation occurs, the woman is not pregnant and, therefore, destroying the "pre-embryo" or preventing it from implanting is not an abortion. This is classic abortion industry jibberish. There is no such thing as a "pre-embryo" and even if there were it would not change a thing. You could invent the term "pre-adult" to describe teenagers, but that wouldn't change the fact that they are human beings.

Why are the same people who oppose abortion always against sex education and birth control?

The pro-life movement has never been opposed to sex education and, in fact, there are pro-life and pro-family organizations all over America working to get sex education into the public school system. What we are opposed to is the kind of sex education programs which have caused America's current epidemic of teen pregnancy, sexually transmitted disease, and abortion. Planned Parenthood and similar organizations are constantly trying to shift the blame for their failed social experiments onto us. They want the public to perceive our opposition to their brand of sex education as the cause of today's teenage pregnancy problem. To see what real hogwash this is, just look at the facts.

In the sixties, groups like Planned Parenthood began to promote a version of sex education in the public schools based on two fundamental concepts. First, it had to be what they called "value neutral" and second, it had to teach that pregnancy prevention is based on contraception rather than abstinence. They contended that the way to reduce the, then, relatively small teen pregnancy rate was to separate morality from sex and teach kids the mechanics of having sexual relationships without getting pregnant. Of course, as any rational human being could predict, if you teach teenagers about sex while leaving the morality component out, you are in effect telling them that there is no morality component to sex. It doesn't take a rocket scientist to figure out that such a message is guaranteed to increase the rate at which they are sexually active.

Planned Parenthood's sales pitch for leaving morality out of sex education is that teaching sexual morality is the responsibility of parents. However, Planned Parenthood originally sold America on the idea of sex education in the public schools by saying that parents don't talk to their kids about sex. The question is, if parents weren't talking to their kids about sex before it was taught in the schools, what was going to make them start doing so afterward? The other question is how this approach is viewed by children living in homes where the parents do talk about sexual morality. What kind of message is sent to those kids when their parents teach them that pre-marital sex is wrong, while their teachers are telling them that pre-marital sex is neither right nor wrong?

Then there is the issue of contraception. Those who advocate the value-neutral, contraception-based approach say that if birth control was taught and adhered to, teen pregnancy would not be a problem. This flies in the face of real-world experience. Public schools began introducing this value-neutral, contraception-based experiment in the mid-sixties and it continues to this day. What we now know is that during this time a relatively small teen pregnancy problem exploded into an epidemic of promiscuity, teen pregnancy, abortion, and sexually transmitted diseases. We're also seeing that children are having sex at much younger ages. Forty years ago, for an 11-year-old girl to be pregnant would have been front-page news. Today, it is not even unusual.

Amazingly, liberal social engineers continue to say that the solution to the problems created by value-neutral, contraception-based sex education is value-neutral, contraception-based sex education. To understand how absurd this is, imagine that during a president's term the American economy experienced a total meltdown. After four years, that person would be looking for a new job. Yet, proponents of value-neutral, contraception-based sex education have produced a meltdown that has lasted almost 40 years while expecting us to keep turning our children over to them.

It is time to stop this insanity. America is like a group of hikers who've discovered that they took a wrong trail. It is time to turn back. It may sound simplistic to say, but the only solution to the catalogue of problems caused by value-neutral, contraception-based sex education is abstinence. It is the only form of birth control and disease prevention that's guaranteed to be effective 100% of the time it's used.

Liberal social engineers claim that abstinence is unrealistic because teenagers are so overwhelmed by raging hormones that they are going to have sex no matter what we do. If that is true, imagine that a teenage girl tells her parents that she is not interested in having sex before marriage but that her boyfriend is really pressuring her to do so. Should her parents tell her that she is being unrealistic to expect him to be abstinent until they are married? Should they advise her to either jump in bed with him or just accept that he will go out and have sex with other girls? Or what if a teenage girl tearfully tells her mother that her boyfriend dumped her because she wouldn't have sex with him? Should the mom tell her that with her next boyfriend she should give in because it is unrealistic to expect boys to be abstinent? What about a teenage girl who says her boyfriend forced her to have sex, would her parents say that she was being unrealistic to expect him to be abstinent?

Obviously, no decent parent would say these things to their daughter. They would tell her that abstinence is entirely reasonable. So the question is, are abstinence-based programs unrealistic? They obviously are not. If it is realistic for a teenage boy to abstain because his girlfriend doesn't want to have sex, then it is just as realistic for him to abstain simply because he has been taught that it is the right thing to do. The argument that kids are going to have sex no matter what we do is a lie. The most that can be said is that some kids will have sex no matter what we do.

Today, many of these liberal social engineers recognize that they are caught between a rock and a hard place. They abhor the abstinence philosophy, but they also see it gaining popularity among parents who've recognized that value-neutral, contraception-based sex education has been a train wreck. Today, the liberal response to the abstinence threat is to push what they call "Abstinence Plus" or "Comprehensive Sex Education." They claim to support teaching abstinence, as long as it is an addition to value-neutral, contraception-based sex education instead of its replacement. In an effort to appear reasonable, some have even conceded that abstinence should be primary.

This is a scam. These people realize that when abstinence-based sex education and value-neutral, contraception-based sex education are combined, the effectiveness of teaching abstinence evaporates. That is because, with teenagers, mixed messages are always dangerous. For example, consider the consequences if parents said the following things to their teenagers:

> "It is best that you don't drink and drive, but if you're going to, don't spill anything on the seats."

> "You're not old enough to be smoking, but if you're going to, be sure to use filtered cigarettes."

> "Your mom and I would prefer that you not take a gun to school, but if you do, all we ask is that you keep the safety on and not point it at anyone."

> "We really don't want you using heroin, but if you are going to, just don't leave any needles lying around where your little brother can get them."

> "Look, I'm telling you not to drive my new Corvette while I'm out of town, but if you do, be sure to replace the gas you use."

Every parent knows what would happen if they said these things to their children. But that is precisely what we're doing when we teach abstinence along side value-neutral, contraception-based sex education. Some might argue that when the focus is solely on abstinence, kids who don't buy the abstinence message are at a higher risk for pregnancy, diseases, and abortion. There may be some validity to that argument. Unfortunately, solving the social problems created by 40 years of value-neutral, contraception-based sex education is not going to be painless. This failed social experiment has put America in the position of having to make some really tough decisions. Our epidemic of teen pregnancy, abortion and sexually transmitted disease was led by a dramatic increase in sexual activity among children, and all the condoms and birth control pills in the world will not turn that around. It is a matter of numbers. The only solution is to reduce the sexual activity of our children, and a mixed message will not do that any more than a mixed message will reduce the chances that a teenage boy will sneak off in his father's new Corvette.

For those who say that the abstinence-only message writes off those children who don't remain abstinent, think about this analogy. When laws requiring children to be strapped into child safety seats were being debated, it was already accepted that some children would be killed because they were in these seats. For example, when cars accidentally go into a river or lake, some children will drown when their parents panic and can't get them out of their car seats. Other children will die in car fires because their parents were rendered unconscious during the wreck and not available to get them out of the car seat. In some crashes, children who would have been thrown from cars and survived, will instead die because they were strapped into a car seat.

The people who wrote the laws requiring car seats for children knew of these risks. But when they voted for these laws, they were not saying, "We're just going to write off all those children who will die because they were in a car seat." Instead, they were simply people who recognized that child safety seats save more lives than they take. In a perfect world they would be able to pass a law to save every child who gets into a car wreck. Unfortunately, they don't live in such a world and so they had to pass a law that would save the most lives possible. Are children dead today who would have been alive if this legislation had not been passed? Absolutely. But far more are alive because of it. In other words, it was a matter of numbers.

That is the same dynamic at play for those of us who advocate abstinence-only sex education. Until we live in a perfect world, we too have to play the numbers. Abstinence-only education will not save every child, but it will save the most children. One thing we know for certain, the very definition of insanity is to think that the value-neutral, contraception-based sex education philosophy which got America into this mess will now get us out of it.

•••

Since we now have over 30 years experience proving that value-neutral, contraception-based sex education does not work, the question is why organizations like Planned Parenthood continue to push it. The answer is that for Planned Parenthood it didn't fail. It accomplished exactly what it was designed to accomplish. To this day, it provides a steady stream of customers for their "reproductive health care" centers.

For those who have a hard time believing that Planned Parenthood would actually try to increase teenage pregnancy, consider this. Back in the fifties and sixties, Planned Parenthood types were constantly whining about the so-called "double standard." They said it was unfair for society to label sexually active girls as tramps while sexually active boys were just macho, red-blooded, all-American boys sowing their wild oats. Undoubtedly, most people would agree with them on that point. However, it was their solution to this issue which exposes their real agenda. When America naively turned its children over to Planned Parenthood, these people didn't go into the nation's classrooms and advocate higher standards for boys, but that society should be willing to accept lower standards from girls.

Looking back, it is now clear why they took this approach. Unplanned pregnancies are a big business and no industry eliminates its own customers. Planned Parenthood wanted to become the nation's abortionist, and they realized that higher standards from boys would result in fewer customers, while lower standards from girls would guarantee more. For Planned Parenthood, value-neutral, contraception-based sex education was not a social policy as much as a business plan. These people knew that the "value-neutral" part of the plan would increase teen sexual activity more than the "contraception-based" part would lower teen pregnancy, and the difference between the two would be teen pregnancies which they could turn into money in the bank.

Unfortunately, the plan worked. Today, the double standard is history. Teenage girls are now as free to be sexually promiscuous as teenage boys. The predictable result is an epidemic of teen pregnancy, abortion and sexually transmitted disease—all of which have been a financial bonanza for Planned Parenthood. Every year Planned Parenthood rakes in hundreds of millions in tax dollars to patch up the problems which their value-neutral, contraception-based sex education created in the first place. Someone would have to be incredibly naive to think that money is not a factor in their continued advocacy of a social experiment which has so undeniably failed.

For those gullible enough to believe that Planned Parenthood would not inflict this sort of misery on children for financial gain, let them remember that alcohol and tobacco manufacturers have knowingly targeted their advertising toward children for decades. What makes anyone think that one large multi-national corporation would market their harmful product toward kids and another one wouldn't? The "reproductive health care" industry has exactly the same motive for targeting children as the tobacco and alcohol industries have. In all three cases, children represent an enormous market that is easily seduced by their products.

The fact is, since we began pushing abortion, contraception, and value-neutral sex education, teen pregnancy and related issues like teenage suicide, sexually transmitted diseases and high school dropout rates have soared. Before then, we didn't routinely hear of 11 and 12-year-old girls getting pregnant and our high schools didn't need day care facilities for the children of their students. Another issue not to be overlooked is the fact that having abortion available when birth control fails, does not protect teenage girls it makes them easier to be sexually exploited. This is clearly evident when pro-life speakers visit schools to talk with teenagers about abortion. It is inevitably the boys who most viciously defend abortion. These guys figured out a long time ago that, for them, abortion serves as a sales tool to talk girls into having sex in the first place, and a safety net to avoid responsibility if their girlfriends end up pregnant.

Legalized abortion also makes it easier for older men to sexually exploit young girls. Contrary to what most people probably believe, our high teen pregnancy rate is not being driven by children having sex with children. America is now experiencing an epidemic of adult men preying on underage girls for sex. According to the most reliable studies, among girls 15 and younger who become pregnant, between 60% and 80% of them are impregnated by adult men. Today, we have reached the point where a junior high school girl is more likely to become pregnant by an adult than by someone close to her own age.

The data also shows that when underage girls become sexually involved with adult men they are exposed to a devastating array of physical and emotional injuries. These illicit relationships set them up to be life-long victims who tend to view their self-worth solely in terms of sex. When compared to girls who are sexually active with boys near their own age, these girls are more likely to:

- have multiple sex partners
- engage in dangerous sexual behaviors
- become pregnant
- drop out of school
- run away from home
- abuse drugs or alcohol
- end up on welfare
- be estranged from friends and family
- be in physically abusive relationships
- become divorced
- be lured into prostitution

Other data shows that among sexually active girls between 11 and 13, those who are having sexual relationships with men more than five years older than themselves are more likely to attempt suicide. Another consequence is that underage girls involved with adult men suffer from sexually transmitted diseases at a far higher rate than girls having sex with boys close to their own age. Studies now show that the highest rate of sexually transmitted diseases in America is found among sexually active females ages 15 to 19, and that the overwhelming majority of these girls contracted these diseases from adult males.

We now know that a major contributor to this tragedy is the fact that the abortion industry protects the men who prey on underage girls. In all 50 states, sexual activity with underage children is illegal. Also, every state mandates that if a healthcare worker has reason to suspect that an underage girl is being sexually abused they are required by law to report that information to a designated law enforcement or child protective services agency. If an underage girl is seeking a pregnancy test, an abortion, birth control or treatment for a sexually transmitted disease, that is evidence of sexual activity by someone who is not old enough to consent to sexual activity. That is reasonable suspicion of sexual abuse and, therefore, triggers the mandated reporting requirement.

At Life Dynamics, we have an overwhelming body of evidence showing that the rate at which the abortion industry fails to comply with mandatory reporting laws is in excess of 90%. This data was obtained from government sources, medical journals, independent researchers, the abortion industry itself, and an undercover investigation which we conducted. (For more information go to ChildPredators.com or contact Life Dynamics for a free printed report on this issue.)

The bottom line is, in order to sell as many abortions as possible the abortion industry has made a conscious decision to conceal the sexual exploitation of children and protect the men who commit these crimes. Once again, we see that legalized abortion doesn't serve or protect women, it serves the abortion industry and sexually predatory males. You can also be assured that if boys and men were the ones who might end up under the abortionist's knife facing unknown emotional and physical risks, they'd have some radically different attitudes about recreational sex and abortion. Of course, these guys don't have to worry about that since their girlfriends submit to the risks all by themselves.

Abortion is only used in certain unavoidable circumstances. It is not used as birth control.

When the abortion lobby was originally selling the idea of making abortion legal, they ridiculed those who said it would one day be used as birth control. They said abortion would only be used in very rare cases and as a one-time safety net for those few women who "made a mistake" or were victims of difficult pregnancies.

Today, even statistics put out by pro-abortion organizations like The Alan Guttmacher Institute, as well as those published by the U.S. Government's Centers for Disease Control, have proven that is a lie. The data from these groups show that, (a) only a tiny percentage of abortions are done for the so-called "hard cases" such as rape, incest, life-of-the-mother, and fetal anomalies, (b) approximately half of all abortions are repeat abortions, and (c) about 35% of all American women of child-bearing age will have had at least one abortion by age 45. It is now undeniable that abortion has become birth control.

Given that, abortion apologists have switched gears and are now selling the idea that even if abortion is used as birth control it's no one else's business.

Of course, it is our business. Since abortion has been legal, the taxpayer has been forced to bear the financial burden of a skyrocketing pregnancy rate among the poor as well as among unmarried teenagers. In short, legalized abortion has proven to be not only morally indefensible, but also a financial disaster.

It is now clear that many sexually active people are less concerned about pregnancy because they rely on abortion as back-up birth control. The flaw with that attitude is that supporting legal abortion as an abstract philosophy is far easier than actually having one. When they're not pregnant, a woman can dismiss the unborn as nothing but a ball of cells or fetal tissue or the product of conception. But when they become pregnant, their natural maternal instincts tell them otherwise. At that point, abortion is no longer as easy an option as it once appeared, and a baby is born which would have never been created had abortion not been relied upon as a safety net. If the mother is unable to support herself or her child, it's going to be the taxpayer who is forced to do so, and that is precisely what is going on in America today.

Why do you oppose fetal tissue research and embryonic stem cell research when so many lives could be saved?

Like any compassionate people, pro-lifers fully support legitimate medical research. However, there is no more evil or dangerous force on earth than science without morality. Whether fetal tissue research or embryonic stem cell research is morally acceptable or not is totally dependent on how the tissue and cells are obtained. If the material comes from babies who died in some natural manner (miscarriage, stillbirth, etc.) there are few people who would raise a moral objection to it being used.

America crossed the line, however, when it began using material from babies who were intentionally killed by abortion. The fact that these children are already dead, or are going to be killed whether we harvest them or not, is irrelevant. It is immoral for a society to profit from slaughtering children. We crossed the line even further when we began actually creating human life for the purpose of destroying it and using it in medical research. These are the practices to which the pro-life community objects. And if the American people think there won't be a day of reckoning over this sort of behavior, then they are living in a state of profound denial.

•••

onmessage

Let's say that a team of researchers developed a drug that would cure cancer, heart disease, and diabetes. In clinical trials, they proved that the drug was not only 100% effective but 100% safe as well. This miracle drug is produced from a chemical found in healthy people between the ages of 15 and 25 years old. These researchers also calculate that the amount of drugs needed to treat the entire country could be produced by taking the chemical from only about 500 donors per year. The downside is that harvesting this chemical always results in the death of the donor.

Given that millions of people could be saved, should we create a national yearly lottery system to select 500 people from the necessary donor group to be killed to make the drug? Think about it. Because only 500 people are needed out of a population pool of millions, each individual's chances of being selected are tiny. Besides, some of those chosen would have died in accidents or illness anyway, and a certain number would not have led very productive lives.

Pragmatically, doesn't it make sense to sacrifice a small handful of these people every year in order to save millions from the horror of cancer, heart disease and diabetes? Of course it does, provided we are willing to say that where the chemical came from is irrelevant. With fetal tissue and embryonic stem cell research, that is precisely what we say about the unborn. So how can we reconcile forcing the unborn into a lottery we wouldn't enter ourselves? All we have to do is focus on the good and not count the cost, and everything will work out fine.

Don't for a moment think that something like this is too far-fetched to happen. If we could go back 50 years and tell people what's happening today in the field of medical research and bio-technology, their response would be to call us insane. They would never have believed that the things we see happening every day all around us would ever be tolerated in this country. Today, hardly a month goes by in which we don't hear of situations no one could possibly have imagined in the past. The only question is where the line will be drawn, and what we will have justified waiting for it to be drawn. Only a fool would believe that we are at any place other than the tip of this iceberg.

When a pro-lifer's daughter gets pregnant, it is amazing how often they become pro-choice.

First, to suggest that this situation is common is an outright lie. However, there is no denying that it does happen occasionally. That's because pro-lifers are human and subject to the same weaknesses as any other human being. Actually, that's just one more reason why the pro-life position is correct. The fact that even people who know it is murder will submit to it under the right circumstances, just proves that unborn children must have their lives protected by law.

Second, let's say that Congress passes a law against insider stock trading and a congressman who voted for the legislation is later found guilty of insider stock trading. Does that mean the law was wrong? What about a police officer who is convicted of robbery, does that mean robbery should be legal since even some police officers commit robberies? Those assertions are no more ridiculous than saying we shouldn't have laws protecting the unborn because a few pro-lifers have taken their daughters for abortions.

Why don't pro-lifers join with us to find ways to end the need for abortion? Let's set aside our differences and look for common ground.

Let's start by getting rid of this fairy tale that abortions are done for "need." Even studies conducted by hardcore abortion advocates prove that almost every abortion performed in America is for non-medical reasons and involves a healthy baby who was not conceived in either rape or incest, and a healthy woman whose pregnancy does not threaten either her life or health. In other words, virtually every abortion performed in America is for want, not need. The fact is, the only people who "need" abortion are the

119

abortionists. To say that we should help them reduce the "need" for abortion, is the same as some pimp asking the vice squad to help him reduce the "need" for prostitution. When the abortion industry abandons their advocacy of abortion, we can talk. Until then, we have nothing in common with anyone who advocates the torture and slaughter of helpless babies. Nor are we looking for any. Our job is to stop these people, not join hands with them.

Why do conservatives want the government to take away a citizen's right to make her own choices?

Conservatism has never meant "anything goes." The basic tenant of conservatism is that the primary reason for government to exist is to protect the lives of those being governed. That remains true whether their lives are threatened by those within the country or those from the outside. It is a perversion for someone to suggest that freedom from government intervention is defined by the government's willingness to look the other way while one human being kills another.

Why is it that conservatives who call themselves pro-life support every war that comes along?

Because there are tens of millions of pro-lifers in America, whenever war is contemplated there are naturally going to be many opinions on both sides of the issue. Regarding the various wars which have occurred since the battle over abortion began, some very conservative pro-lifers have been quite outspoken in their opposition to America's involvement.

•••

To suggest that if someone is pro-life it is out of place for them to also support their country's decision to go to war, is irrational given that there is no similarity between the participants. One is a full grown, highly trained, armed to the teeth adult who volunteered to be a soldier in the American military. He is confronting an enemy which our government has determined—rightly or wrongly— poses a threat to our country. The other is an innocent baby helplessly lying in its mother's womb, posing no threat and the enemy of no one. Additionally, the decision to go to war is one that is carried out in public with often heated debate by people on both sides of the issue. Contrary to what some people would have you believe, the decision for America to go to war is never the unilateral decision of one person. The opposition gets to make its case. They can appeal directly to the American people or to their elected officials, they can try to stop the funding for the war or they can go to court to stop it.

In the case of abortion, there is no debate. If for any reason whatsoever or no reason whatsoever, the mother decides to kill her child—that child is doomed. No one else has a legal way to stop the killing. If abortion defenders want to make an analogy between war and abortion, perhaps our country should require the same standards for having an abortion that we require for going to war. Until we do that, there is no analogy.

Why is it that pro-lifers talk about the sanctity of human life while supporting the death penalty?

To begin with, there are many pro-life people who don't support the death penalty. However, those who do are not disqualified from legitimately claiming to be pro-life. It is not inconsistent to contend that convicted murderers should be executed but innocent babies should not be. It is interesting that while the pro-choice crowd sees opposing abortion and supporting the death penalty as hypocritical, they see people who support abortion for the innocent while opposing the death penalty for the guilty as enlightened. That is the very definition of hypocrisy.

•••

If these people see abortion and capital punishment as the same, wouldn't they want to see each applied in the same way? The Constitution says that no one should be deprived of life, liberty or property without due process of law. So when a mom wants an abortion, let's charge her baby with being inconvenient, unwanted, too expensive, unhealthy or whatever crime warrants its death. At trial the mom can testify as to why her child is deserving of death and she could even bring in witnesses to confirm her story. On the defense side, perhaps a family willing to adopt the child could be permitted to speak on its behalf. If the verdict is that this baby is indeed a menace, following the same mandatory appeal process given to other condemned prisoners, the child would be executed.

Of course, abortion defenders are going to scoff at this because they never saw a legitimate analogy between abortion and capital punishment in the first place. Even they recognize that people executed by lethal injection have been convicted of a horrible murder, while people executed by abortion have harmed no one. Any way you cut it, the pro-choice mob is all for giving a trial to an ax-murderer, but not to a child. On the other hand, pro-lifers are asking for the innocent to have at least as much protection as the guilty. The bottom line is, abortion means no judge, no jury, no trial, no appeal and no stay of execution, and that is exactly how the abortion industry likes it.

•••

In January of 2000, the governor of Illinois issued a moratorium on the death penalty citing concerns that the state may execute an innocent person. Politicians all across America—many of them rabid defenders of legalized abortion—lauded this action and called for other governors to follow suit. The question is, where is the moratorium on abortion? Why is a nation that is, appropriately, unwilling to take the smallest chance of executing even one innocent human being in the gas chamber, so unwilling to consider the possibility that it may be executing millions of innocent human beings in the womb?

How can you people call yourselves pro-life when your movement is so violent? Just look at all the doctors who've been murdered.

To begin with, the level of violence committed by people opposed to abortion has been grotesquely exaggerated by both the abortion lobby as well as their media lapdogs. In over 30 years, three abortionists and four other abortion clinic employees have been killed. It must also be pointed out that not one of these killings occurred prior to the inauguration of Bill Clinton. Immediately after taking office, he and his Attorney General, Janet Reno, began paying off their campaign debts to the abortion lobby. While Clinton got legislation passed that was specifically designed to sweep the streets clean of peaceful non-violent picketers, Reno secretly turned the Attorney General's office and the FBI into a private police force for the abortion industry.

> **NOTE:** When rumors about these witch-hunts began, Reno publically denied their existence. However, government documents were eventually made public that proved she had been lying. In fact, it was revealed that this campaign even had a name. It was called VAAPCON.

Given this environment, it is hardly surprising that less than three months after Clinton and Reno began cracking skulls, the first shooting occurred. This is not to suggest that the environment justifies the violence, but we cannot act as if the violence occurred in a vacuum. When a woman murders her abusive husband, we may agree that the abuse did not justify the murder, but we would certainly understand that it may have been a motivating factor. In this case, given that no shootings occurred until after the Clinton/Reno inquisition began, it would be illogical to ignore it.

The abortion lobby likes to paint this picture of besieged doctors living in constant fear of being murdered, with survival requiring that they arm themselves to the teeth, install million-dollar security systems, and employ around-the-clock bodyguards. This is nothing more than grandstanding to gain public and political sympathy for the moral degenerates who work at abortion clinics.

Look at the facts. When the Department of Justice or the FBI publish studies on workplace violence, the rate of violence at abortion clinics is so statistically insignificant that is doesn't even make it into the final reports. In fact, so few abortionists are killed that even if you limit the statistics to only include health care professionals, abortionists are still not on the radar screen.

Even if you focus on the time period during which the most pro-life violence occurred, it is immediately clear how overblown this issue has been. In 1993 and 1994, five abortion clinic workers were killed. However, according to U.S. government statistics published by the National Institute for Occupational Safety and Health (NIOSH), during those same two years there were 2,154 other people killed in work-related homicides in the United States. This included, 7 school teachers, 4 members of the clergy, 10 lawyers, 9 newspaper vendors, 7 writers, 6 realtors, 22 waiters or waitresses, 40 garage or service station attendants, 4 groundskeepers, 5 architects, 23 auto mechanics, 10 hairdressers, 4 carpenters, 21 janitors, and 6 farmers.

That's right. Even during the worst period of pro-life violence in American history, **more farmers** and **twice as many hairdressers** were murdered on the job than abortion clinic workers and abortionists combined. And remember, the five abortion clinic killings during 1993 and 1994 account for all but two of the killings that have happened in the entire 30-plus year history of the pro-life movement. In other words, during the other 30 years only two people were murdered. Compared to the thousands of taxi drivers, convenience store employees, policemen, firemen, and others who were killed during that time, it is clear that the abortion mill is an incredibly safe environment for its employees.

This image of abortion workers having to dodge a hail of automatic weapon fire just to get from their car to the clinic door is utter nonsense. The reason it seems otherwise is because when some poor guy is gunned down behind the counter of a convenience store, the story gets buried on page 12 in the Metro section of the paper. But when an abortionist gets shot, it is the lead story on every national and local newscast in America, at least one of the national "news magazine" shows will rush out a *Special Report* cataloguing pro-life violence, pro-lifers will be rounded up, Justice Department news conferences will be held, Congressional hearings will be scheduled, new legislation will be introduced, and hundreds of federal marshalls will be stationed at the nation's abortion mills.

Then, the abortion industry's legion of media stooges will make sure the issue stays in front of the public. For the next few years, every article about abortion is certain to include a mention of this shooting and other pro-life violence—whether real or imagined. Also, media reports on terrorism anywhere in the world will often include references to "domestic terrorists like those who target abortion clinics." This particular tactic has been used extensively since the 9/11 attacks. When the media has been forced to report that an act of terrorism was linked to Muslim fundamentalists, they have inevitably used it as an opportunity to remind the public about "pro-life Christian fundamentalists who shoot doctors for providing legal reproductive health care services."

If the scenario I've described above seems exaggerated, be assured it is not. This is precisely how the pro-life movement's reputation for violence was manufactured. Overlooked in all this is the fact that the media is able to make such a big deal about pro-life violence only because it is so incredibility rare. If it were even remotely common, there is no way they could give it so much press. It's like airline crashes. They are newsworthy because they happen so infrequently. If airliners routinely crashed, media reports about them would end up on the same page as stories about employees killed at convenience stores.

Also overlooked is the fact that if abortion clinic shootings, assaults, bombings, arson and other acts of violence were anywhere near as common as the abortion lobby claims, there would not be one insurance company in America that would sell them coverage.

The reality is, the pro-life movement is, and has always been, the most peaceful socio-political movement of its size and tenure in American history. To see the truth of that, all one has to do is study the other causes which are most similar: the anti-slavery, civil rights, and labor struggles. The **cumulative total** of all the violence which has occurred in the 30-plus year history of the pro-life movement, does not even remotely compare to many **single incidences** of violence which have often occurred in those movements.

The fact that the Ku Klux Klan is pro-life shows just what kind of bigots oppose legal abortion.

Is this to say that the millions of Americans who identify themselves as pro-life are the same as the Ku Klux Klan? To appreciate how abysmally stupid this is, imagine it was revealed that a notorious child molester happened to be a Democrat. Would the public buy a Republican argument that there is a relationship between being a member of the Democratic Party and molesting children? Or let's assume the Klan issued a statement today saying it opposes adultery. Does that mean that adultery is good because the Klan is against it? If a local pastor speaks out against adultery, should we assume that he parades around the woods at night with a sheet over his head?

Actually, what abortion defenders need to be thinking about is that even Klansmen have enough morals to be against the killing of children. That may not say very much about the Klan, but it says volumes about the pro-choice crowd.

Abortion should be safe, legal, and rare.

If legalized abortion is such an empowering thing for women, why would we want it to be rare? If it is not the killing of a child, why should its use, even in high numbers, be a problem? And if it is a Constitutional right, why shouldn't it be celebrated? We don't hear anyone saying that free speech or freedom of religion should be rare. Why apply this illogical standard to abortion?

If you don't like abortion, don't have one. It's that simple.

This sort of arrogant statement is only made by cold-blooded cynics who know that their pro-choice position is impossible to defend on its own merits. Of course, the pro-life movement would be perfectly happy with this solution as long as we extend the same offer to the unborn. That only seems fair given that every time a mom has an abortion her baby also has one. Since it seems unlikely that unborn children like abortion, according to this philosophy they should be given the option of not having one.

That brings up an interesting question. Would all the people who call themselves pro-choice still be pro-choice if they were the ones being chosen? If it were possible to transport them back to their mom's wombs, and if it were also possible to interview them there, would they still have this "don't-like-abortion-then-don't-have-one" attitude? Would they still be making such idiotic statements if they were the ones who might be ripped apart alive, ground up in a garbage disposal and flushed down the city sewer system?

Abortion is no big deal. It is a simple five-minute procedure.

So what? A criminal can hold up a convenience store and gun down everyone in the place in far less than five minutes. A drunk driver can kill an entire family in a split second. In five minutes, a woman can be raped and murdered.

All of those are examples of simple procedures that only take a short time to accomplish. So what is the significance of how long an abortion takes?

Imagine that a baby is about to be aborted, but instead of doing it inside the womb the child is taken out alive and placed on a table. Then, the arms are pulled off, the legs are pulled off, the chest is crushed, the skull is collapsed causing the brains to pour out, etc. There will also be a heart monitor hooked up to the child so we can see his heart race as this ex-uterine abortion begins. The only difference between this abortion and the other 3,000 happening today, is that this one is going to be shown live on national television. The question is, would the public's reaction to what they saw be swayed by the fact that it only took five minutes?

127

onmessage

Outlawing abortion will not end it. Women have always had abortions and they always will.

Outlawing rape hasn't stopped it either. Nor has the law stopped all armed robberies, murders, car thefts or any other abhorrent behavior. Does that mean these things should be legal? By abortion industry logic, apparently they should.

Obviously, no one is stupid enough to believe that making abortion illegal will end it. No law ever completely eliminated the activity it was passed to address. Laws are enacted because society has determined that the activity in question is unacceptable behavior. The fact is, if we were to only pass those laws which we know beforehand will be 100% effective we wouldn't have any laws at all.

How can you people justify showing those horrible graphic pictures? It is offensive. Besides, those are not abortions they are stillbirths and miscarriages.

Why would we need phony pictures of stillbirths or miscarriages when dead babies can be found in abortion clinic dumpsters? And where would we get stillborn babies to photograph? Stillborn babies are legally required to be sent to either a funeral home for embalming and burial or cremation.

Additionally, if those dead babies were really stillborn and not aborted, where did all the wounds and torn-off body parts come from? Does anyone seriously believe that hospitals provide us with corpses which we then beat to a pulp, dismember, and photograph?

As for miscarriages, how on earth would we get those? When miscarriages occur at medical facilities, doctors send the material out for a pathology report. Why would a physician jeopardize his medical career, not to mention the life of his patient, by giving the material to the pro-life movement to photograph? Perhaps the pro-choice mob is suggesting that these photos come from women who have had miscarriages at home. That could be. After all, when a woman loses her baby it is probably pretty certain that the first thing she thinks about is alerting the pro-life movement so we can come rushing over with our lights and cameras.

With that idiocy out of the way, the real question is why the abortion lobby gets so hysterical over these pictures. If legal abortion is such a good thing that it should be called a "fundamental Constitutional right," why wouldn't those abortion photos be celebrated? Shouldn't they fill these people with a sense of pride and satisfaction? In fact, why aren't they found in abortion clinic ads or on posters in the offices of pro-choice politicians? If abortion isn't wrong, these photos should be used as proof of what an enlightened and progressive society we are.

It is textbook hypocrisy to object to the pictures of dead babies, but not object to the killing of the babies, and it is not only the pro-life community that recognizes this. In an article, *Our Bodies, Our Souls*, published in *The New Republic* magazine on October 16, 1995, radical pro-abortion author, Naomi Wolf, stated that:

> *"Those photographs are in fact photographs of actual D&Cs; those footprints are in fact the footprints of a 10-week-old fetus; the pro-life slogan, 'Abortion stops a beating heart,' is incontrovertibly true. While images of violent fetal death work magnificently for pro-lifers as political polemic, the pictures are not polemical in themselves: they are biological facts. ... How can we charge that it is vile and repulsive for pro-lifers to brandish vile and repulsive images if the images are real? To insist that the truth is in poor taste is the height of hypocrisy."*

In other words, if you can't take the reality that abortion is chopping up a live baby you have no business defending it. How can someone be offended at a picture of a dead child but approve of the killing? Of course, the pro-choice crowd goes into such a frenzy over these photographs for the same reason they are so terrified at technological advances like 3-D and color ultrasound. Both expose a reality to the American people which the abortion industry has been hiding for more than 30 years.

Ultrasound images transform the argument that the unborn are living human children from a belief into an observable fact. Meanwhile, the graphic photos prove that abortion is the brutal and violent murder of these children. The pro-choice crowd realizes that when the public sees these images, the only way for them to support legalized abortion is to deny what they are seeing with their own eyes. So whether abortion defenders like it or not, the pro-life movement will continue to show pictures of dead babies as long as they keep killing live ones. The fact is, if they weren't killing them we wouldn't have pictures to show.

I've known several women who had abortions and most of them didn't regret it at all.

Adolf Eichmann went to his execution saying he had no regrets about his participation in the Nazi holocaust. Does that make what he did right? Of course not. Lack of regret relates to the conscience of the person acting, not to the rightness of the act itself. If some pervert has sex with his neighbor's five-year-old daughter, whether he regrets it or not is irrelevant.

Doctors don't do abortions for the money. Abortions are only about $300 but a doctor can make several thousand dollars taking a woman through delivery.

First, only the earliest abortions can be bought for $300. Later ones can reach $5,000 to $10,000. But even if an abortionist only does the early ones, it doesn't require a degree in economics to understand that $300 for ten minutes work is more than $5,000 for nine months work. Second, it is laughable to believe that someone whose medical career has reached the point where he has to work at an abortion clinic, is someone any rational woman would allow to deliver her baby. Whatever their political views on abortion, legitimate medical practitioners almost universally agree that abortionists are the washouts, losers and moral degenerates of medicine. Working at an abortion clinic is the last stop before they're out the door. For these guys, the choice is not between doing abortions or delivering babies, but between doing abortions or doing nothing. If not for the abortion business, they'd be washing BMWs not driving them.

I work at an abortion clinic and I can tell you we routinely receive letters from women telling us how grateful they are for the service we provide them.

So what? The man who is having an affair is probably grateful to his neighbors who keep his wife in the dark. The hit-and-run driver who kills a pedestrian is probably grateful to his friends who were in the car with him and never reported his crime to the police. The alcoholic who is always late for work is probably grateful to the co-workers who cover up for him. Gratitude just means that someone did what someone else wanted them to do, not that what they did was morally defensible.

The gratitude of a woman to the hired serial killer she paid to slaughter her child is a textbook example of that phenomenon.

You people are just anti-choice extremists. Keep your Rosaries off my ovaries!

First, when "choice" is defined as the right to butcher helpless children by the millions, you're right. I am anti-choice. If that makes me an extremist, so be it. Second, setting aside the obvious anti-Catholic bigotry, it is curious that radical abortion supporters would connect Rosaries and ovaries given that so many of them are men. That may require a psychiatrist to explain.

Obviously, it is no secret that many abortion opponents are Roman Catholics who pray the Rosary. A significant number might also eat fish on Fridays. So why not, "Keep your flounders off my fallopians?"

onmessage

Returning to earth for a moment, the world can rest assured that we pro-lifers are pretty indifferent to pro-choicers' ovaries—as well as their tonsils, spleens, and gall bladders.

Instead, we want to address the question of whether killing children is something that civilized people do? We also want to talk about the fact that when a woman submits to abortion, a lot of people might be better off but she isn't one of them. It could be the guy who got her pregnant and doesn't want to face his responsibilities, parents who don't want to be embarrassed that their daughter got pregnant, an employer who doesn't want to come in second to a woman's baby, or the abortionist who put her money in his pocket. As for the woman, she went from being the mother of a live baby to the mother of a dead one. It is hard to imagine how she's better off for that experience.

Meanwhile, the pro-choice mob keeps trying to dodge these issues by going off on these bizarre tangents about prayer beads and body organs.

Indexes

onmessage

The government should not be involved in the practice of medicine. 25

•

If our state restricts abortion, women will just go to other states. 25

•

The government has an obligation to fund abortions for poor women. 25

•

I am against abortion, but when I vote I look at all issues. Besides, most elected offices have no impact on abortion. 27

•

Don't get hung up on abortion. Politicians and judges have other issues to deal with and we should not have litmus tests. 27

•

The government has no business telling a woman what she can or can't do with her own body. 28

•

Abortion is about empowering women and allowing them to make their own choices. 29

•

The issue is whether we trust women to be their own moral agents and make good moral decisions. 30

•

This is a woman's issue. Men have no say in whether

women have the right to get an abortion. 32

•

If men could get pregnant, abortion would be a sacrament. 34

•

What you and I believe about abortion is not the point. The issue is, what does the woman believe. 38

•

Women cannot be free unless they have the right to control their own reproductive lives. 39

•

What gives you the right to tell a woman she can't have an abortion? 39

•

If abortion is made illegal, how do women guard against having their miscarriages investigated by the police? How do they prove they didn't actually have an illegal abortion? 39

•

Outlawing abortion will impose an unequal burden on poor women. The wealthy will always be able to go to other countries for abortions. 40

•

The Supreme Court said women have a Constitutional right to privacy, and that includes abortion. Why should a fetus have more rights than

onmessage

the woman? 41

·

I am not for abortion on demand, I support the compromise reached in Roe v. Wade. 44

·

The Supreme Court settled this issue. They said that the fetus is not a person and that abortion is a Constitutional right. 46

·

How can a fetus have Constitutional rights before it is viable? 47

·

How can tissue that is only a quarter of an inch in diameter have Constitutional rights? 48

·

The Constitution says that only people who are "born or naturalized in the United States" have Constitutional rights. So how does a fetus have Constitutional rights? 49

·

Laws prohibiting abortion are relatively new. By English Common Law, abortion was even legal when our Constitution was written. Why should we outlaw it now? 49

·

Why should abortion be outlawed when polls show that the majority of Americans are pro-choice? 49

There is no consensus for making abortion illegal. 50

·

If abortion is illegal, what should the penalty be for a woman who has one? 50

·

How can pro-lifers justify saying abortion should be illegal even when the pregnancy threatens the life of the mother? What about her right to life? 52

·

Why should a woman who was the victim of rape or incest have to bear a child? 54

·

How can you tell a woman whose doctor says her fetus is handicapped that she has to have it? Besides, these children can lead terrible lives. 57

·

No woman ever wanted to have an abortion. They do it because they need to. They have good reasons. 62

·

How can we tell a woman whose baby is going to die anyway that she can't have an abortion? 63

·

I think these abortions where the baby is ripped apart are terrible, but I don't have a problem with the abortion pill. 63

onmessage

What about a single mom who just can't afford another child? 64

·

Pro-lifers talk about late term abortion as if they are common. Late term abortions are never done unless the woman's life is in danger or the baby is either already dead or couldn't survive anyway. 64

·

If abortion is outlawed women will again be forced to back-ally butchers and they will lose their lives. 66

·

You people talk about the dangers of abortion, but abortion is safer than childbirth. 69

·

I am opposed to abortion, but I don't believe I have the right to inflict my personal beliefs on others. 70

·

The answer to abortion is not in making it against the law but in changing hearts. 72

·

You cannot legislate morality. 73

·

You have no right to tell others what to believe. 74

·

What gives you people the right to force your religious beliefs on others? 74

Can someone be pro-choice and a Christian? 75

·

During His ministry, Jesus never spoke out against abortion. 75

·

The Bible does not condemn abortion. 75

·

As a Christian, I know that abortion is wrong, but I don't feel that the Lord is leading me to take a stand on this issue. 76

·

As a Christian, I know abortion is wrong, but God gave us free will. It is not our place to judge a woman who wants to have an abortion. 78

·

Abortion is just one of many issues the church has to be concerned about. The economy, the homeless, the death penalty, U.S. military policy, education, health care, and hunger are important too. 78

·

I know abortion is evil, but my obligation is to save souls, not bodies. Besides, those babies go to heaven anyway. 79

·

When a woman miscarries, are you saying that God did something evil? Is God an abortionist? 80

onmessage

I believe that abortion is wrong, but I also believe that the solution is prayer. 80

•

If a woman just isn't ready for a baby, maybe it's best that she terminate the pregnancy and ask God to bring the child back at a better time. 81

•

Since even theologians can't agree when life begins or when the soul enters the body, why should abortion be illegal? 81

•

No one can prove when life begins. It is up to the woman to decide based on her own beliefs. 82

•

We don't deny that the fetus is potential human life, but that is different from an actual human being. 83

•

Pro-lifers talk about abortion as killing a baby. That is not true. There is a fetus, but no baby. 84

•

Pro-lifers say adoption is the answer, but what about all the black babies that aren't getting adopted right now? 86

•

What about all the children who get adopted by people who abuse or neglect them? 87

Adoption is not the solution. Thousands of children are waiting to be adopted right now. If a baby is not a white, healthy, newborn it stands little chance of being adopted. 88

•

There are more abortions every year than there are people waiting to adopt. What do we do with all those children after these people have gotten the baby they want? 89

•

What about a woman who says she could not handle carrying a child for nine months and then giving it up for adoption? 90

•

What about the emotional damage done to women who give up their babies for adoption? 91

•

Why don't you pro-lifers do something to help people who are already born, like the homeless? 91

•

The world has a major problem with overpopulation. So how would we feed these children when millions are already starving? 94

•

As a taxpayer, I'd rather pay $300 for a welfare mom's

onmessage

abortion than pay thousands of dollars to raise her kid for 18 years. 96

•

I don't want to pay for all the social problems created by people having children they don't want and can't afford. 97

•

Some children lead terrible lives. Wouldn't abortion be better than that? 99

•

What about all the children who will be abused because they were unwanted? We need to make sure that every child is a wanted child. 100

•

Why should a woman who is acting responsibly and using birth control be subjected to forced motherhood just because her birth control failed? 101

•

The best way to prevent abortion is by promoting contraception. 102

•

Why are the same people who oppose abortion always against sex education and birth control? 107

•

Abortion is only used in certain unavoidable circumstances. It is not used as birth control. 116

Why do you oppose fetal tissue research and embryonic stem cell research when so many lives could be saved? 117

•

When a pro-lifer's daughter gets pregnant, it is amazing how often they become pro-choice. 119

•

Why don't pro-lifers join with us to find ways to end the need for abortion? Let's set aside our differences and look for common ground. 119

•

Why do conservatives want the government to take away a citizen's right to make her own choices? 120

•

Why is it that conservatives who call themselves pro-life support every war that comes along? 120

•

Why is it that pro-lifers talk about the sanctity of human life while supporting the death penalty? 121

•

How can you people call yourselves pro-life when your movement is so violent? Just look at all the doctors who've been murdered. 122

•

The fact that the Ku Klux Klan is pro-life shows just what kind

onmessage

SUBJECT INDEX

onmessage

onmessage

onmessage

onmessage

onmessage